Spotlight on Technology
in Education

Spotlight on Technology in Education

Edited by Nancy Walser

No. 7 in the *Harvard Education Letter* Spotlight Series

HARVARD EDUCATION PRESS
CAMBRIDGE, MASSACHUSETTS

Library of Congress Control Number 2010942140

Paperback ISBN 978-1-934742-89-1
Library Edition ISBN 978-1-934742-90-7

Published by Harvard Education Press,
an imprint of the Harvard Education Publishing Group

Harvard Education Press
8 Story Street
Cambridge, MA 02138

Cover Design: Sarah Henderson
The typefaces used in this book are Humanist 777 for text and Kuenstler 480 for display.

Contents

Foreword

Will Richardson

L et's be clear: it's an amazing time to be a learner.
Whether it's the two billion teachers we can now connect to on the Web, the myriad of entertaining and at the same time educational video games we can play with our friends (or by ourselves), or the potential to answer almost any question we can pose through a few keystrokes on the phones in our pockets, we live at a moment of ubiquitous learning, one few of our ancestors could have imagined. It's a moment that in many ways we ourselves are still struggling to make sense of, struggling to imagine the endless possibilities that we find ourselves swimming in.

That my daughter can come home from school one day with the desire to learn to play a new song on the piano, one she'd heard for the first time earlier that day, and two hours later be well on her way to mastering it still boggles my mind. (That it was Journey's "Don't Stop Believin'" was even more disorienting). Her teachers were a YouTube video created by a Journey aficionado, an illegally downloaded set of sheet music (we had "the talk" later), and her own passion to play. No other human in the room needed. In fact, if she had the Magic Piano app for the iPad, no piano needed either. It's a story that's being played out repeatedly every day, around the world, by kids and adults of all ages. We can learn what we want, when we want to, if we have the desire and the connection. More and more of us are finding both.

The Web and its accompanying technologies, as well as the games and mobile devices we're all carrying around, are driving a surge in personalized learning that, ironically, most people alive at the moment still don't even know exists. Sure, most in the developed world have at least heard of Facebook by now, and as more people get access, the idea of social networking online is growing in dramatic spurts around the world. But lost in the thrill of the social connections we can now make with friends past and present have been the opportunities to use these spaces to learn and learn deeply. We live in a world where we can literally create our own *learning* networks in which we pull in content and mentors and collaborators to participate with us. If we know what we're doing, we can create our own classrooms, our own curriculum, and to some extent, fashion our own online learning portfolio for others to evaluate and assess.

All of which, by the way, poses huge challenges for those places our kids go off to each day to learn the stuff that others have deemed important for them to learn. My daughter (and my son) are both getting used to learning what they want to learn, when they want to learn it, with whom they want to learn it, and they're wondering why they can't do more of that in school. I'm wondering that too. That's not to say that we should turn the kids loose and let them Google and game their way to an education on their own. Not at all. But it is to say that what they need schools to prepare them for today is much different than what schools have been preparing students for over the past 100 years or so. In this fast changing moment, my kids don't need so much to be *learned*, a quality the philosopher Eric Hoffer says will render them "equipped to live in a world that no longer exists." Instead, they need to be *learners*, solving real problems, creating new knowledge, and sharing and reflecting on those experiences with others. Unfortunately, that's not what the vast majority of our current schools are about.

In this *Spotlight on Technology in Education*, many of these challenges and opportunities have been compiled into a cogent, thought-provoking collection that asks us to think deeply about the changes we find ourselves in the midst of. It's not just about technology; it's about the learning we can now do with technology and the many considerations that go along with this profound shift to a networked, digital-learning culture. To be sure, it's the tools, the blogs and wikis, the video games, and the virtual environments that ground those shifts. But what is propelling us to a new ecology of learning are the connections and collaborations that those tools afford us. That's where the real possibilities for new learning occur.

These chapters take us into classrooms to consider spaces where both teachers and students are learners and risk-takers, where ideas are introduced and debated, reflected upon, and shared with the world in ways that lead others into the conversation. They are places where all of the players, young and old, are engaged not just in disseminating and assessing old knowledge but instead in creating and collaborating with others to produce and publish new understandings of their worlds. They are places in which a "fundamental re-conception" of traditional structures is taking place and new environments for learning are blossoming.

In addition, this collection paints a compelling picture of the use of video games to teach deeply, not just content but also the fundamental learning literacies of this age: self-direction, self-assessment, reflection, perseverance, focus, and drive. And it also broaches the coming wave of using games to assess what students can actually do with what they have learned, an outcome very few of the traditional standardized assessments can adequately measure. There can be little doubt that much of our learning future will include gaming environments to teach and to assess.

But a compilation such as this would be incomplete without a rigorous examination of the challenges to the changes being discussed. In general, how do we have to think differently about assessment? How do we prepare teachers for their changing roles and expectations in the classroom? What are the very important questions around access and equity that every educator needs to think about? And finally, what does all of this mean for the traditional conceptions we have of schools as the dominant part of our learning experience?

In as much as a concise collection of 12 essays can, this Spotlight offers an exceedingly well-rounded launching pad for those questions and many more as we begin to more fully imagine where we can go as learners with these new globally networked technologies. If we are to truly prepare our children for the learning lives that they are going to lead, as opposed to the ones most of us grew up with, we need to begin fashioning the answers that will lead us as individuals and systems to a very different place. This book is a great place to start.

Introduction

Nancy Walser

As we enter the second decade of the 21st century, it may seem a little strange to single out technology as a discrete topic for an education book. We are rapidly approaching—if we have not already reached—an era where computers, cell phones, iPods, and e-readers are as ubiquitous as pencils in today's classrooms. Like pencils, these technological tools may someday hardly seem worthy of special attention.

But for now, the world is more complicated. The very rapidity with which these new tools have entered the classroom has meant that teachers and students are grappling with changes, both large and small, to the established order. Every educator—not just the media specialist—must now be technologically savvy. Oftentimes, they are making things up as they go; research into the most effective ways to use these tools in K–12 schools is still very much in its infancy.

Many of these tools lead to the Internet, of course—a resource that is a double-edged sword. By now, educators are highly aware that the online world is a place where both constructive and destructive forces are unleashed, enhancing our most creative human impulses and exposing the worst. Teachers who can steer their students around the pitfalls and show them how to use the Internet safely and productively are way ahead of the game.

But harnessing the Internet for learning is only one slice of what technology offers education. As you will read in these pages, technology may hold the key to important break-throughs in both policy and practice. Can computer tests, for example, finally allow state testing systems to go beyond standard multiple-choice questions to assess those all-important critical thinking skills? Will "hybrid" schools that strive to combine the best of online and face-to-face instruction finally free teachers up to become facilitators of student-directed learning? Can video games allow teachers to document the creative choices students make as they attempt to solve real-world problems that make learning more relevant and, perhaps, even fun?

For several years, the *Harvard Education Letter* has been exploring the promises and challenges of technology use in schools. This volume, the seventh anthology in the *Harvard Education Letter* Spotlight Series, brings together 12 articles that examine technology use in three major areas: the classroom, assessment, and school improvement. These topics form the three sections in this volume.

The first section, "Technology in the Classroom," begins with three chapters by education journalist Colleen Gillard. In the opening chapter, Gillard covers the fundamentals of using the Internet for research beginning in the middle school years. Citing expert librarians, media specialists, and teachers, Gillard pinpoints three essential skills that students need to acquire to do effective online searches, evaluation of sources, and citations as well as strategies that educators have found to be effective in helping students acquire these skills. Explicit instruction on proper attribution of sources is especially important since the ease of cutting and pasting from the Web has been linked to a documented increase in plagiarism.

The Web also offers a wealth of free tools to help teachers enhance their classroom teaching. Chapter 2 looks at how teachers use blogs, wikis, and podcasts to engage students in and out of the classroom. Chapter 3 focuses specifically on strategies for using "dumb" cell phones, since the costs of data plans for smart phones are still out of reach for many families.

In addition to computers and cell phones, teachers are using tools such as digital cameras and Global Positioning Systems (GPS) to teach 21st century skills like critical thinking. Chapter 4 presents extended examples of these kinds of activities from real classrooms across the United States. These examples show that there are really no limits to the creative use of technological tools to enhance even the most typical lesson plan.

Finally, in a provocative and prescient essay, Arizona State University professor James Paul Gee lays out an argument for why educators should look to well-designed video games when attempting to create more stimulating learning environments. "Why is it," he asks, "that many children can't sit still long enough to finish their homework and yet will spend hours playing games on the computer?" The answer doesn't lie in the entertainment value of video games as much as in the evidence that they tap into things that naturally motivate young learners: like context, choice, and challenge, he argues. Since the publication of this essay, several schools featuring adaptive "game-like" curricula that tailor learning for individual students have opened (see chapter 11).

THE PROMISE OF BETTER ASSESSMENTS

Two decades into the standards movement, educators are still grappling with the problem of how to create assessments that go beyond multiple-choice questions that simply measure basic skills. Technology—hand-held devices and computers, in particular—may hold the key to breakthroughs in these areas.

In chapter 6, Robert Rothman, a frequent contributor to the *Harvard Education Letter*, takes an in-depth look at the benefits and limitations of computer testing in Oregon, the first state where nearly all students take required state tests on a computer.

In chapter 7, Rothman explores the work of researchers who are developing a new generation of assessments that use video games as their model, while creating data that teachers may someday be able to use to measure 21st century skills such as critical thinking, problem-solving ability, communication, and scientific inquiry skills. And in chapter 8, Rothman looks at the more immediate possibilities for widespread use of computer tests in 44 states and the District of Columbia that have tentatively (as of this writing) signed up to use one of two new testing systems as early as 2014.

THE CHANGING FACE OF SCHOOLING

The final section of this book, "Technology and School Improvement," looks at a variety of ways reformers are using technology not just to improve teaching and learning, but sometimes to change the very essence of what "school" means. Chapter 9 profiles several school systems that adopted one-to-one laptop programs and examines the implications and benefits for both teachers and students. In chapter 10, Kristina Cowan traces the blossoming of the virtual schools movement and the early efforts to guide and assess the quality of online learning, while in chapter 11, Brigid Schulte looks at the emerging "bricks and clicks" schools—so called hybrid schools—that are combining online learning with traditional "face-to-face" (F2F) teaching.

While the Internet has opened up a world of resources for teachers to use with their students, it is also opening up a new world for teacher training. In the final chapter of this book, Dave Saltman looks at the proliferation of online websites supporting professional development, and specifically how this trend is helping teach both teachers and students how to better collaborate.

"Digital learning is like a thoroughbred racehorse. You can't keep it locked up in a stable. It's going to get out," says former West Virginia Governor Bob Wise, who is now leading the Digital Learning Council with former Florida Governor Jeb Bush. While technology is now a given in education, these chapters not only illustrate how much promise it offers, but how much there is yet to be learned. Technology use is bound to grow in schools—of this most experts are sure—but which developments will be most constructive, engaging, motivating, and effective for which individuals and groups? These chapters are meant to offer an overview of the expanding options for educators, who will influence the role of technology in the classrooms of the future.

PART I

Technology in the Classroom

CHAPTER 1

Internet Research 101

How to help middle school students avoid getting tangled up in the Web

Colleen Gillard

Evanston, Ill., eighth-grade humanities teacher Claudia Garrison has seen it all: the paper citing "Michael" (as in Michael Jackson) as a source for infant mortality statistics; the paper whose different fonts unwittingly revealed where material had been cut and pasted from the Web; and the paper whose expert opinion came from a blog.

Fast and convenient, the World Wide Web has become an unparalleled informational resource. It surpasses the card catalogue as the main entry point for students embarking on papers and projects. However, it poses particular problems for beginning researchers. Students need to learn new skills to find the information they need, evaluate it appropriately, and distinguish between others' work—properly credited—and their own.

The dramatic rise in plagiarism—whether intentional or unintentional—indicates the urgent need to train students in good Internet research skills. As many as one-third of college papers written today are marred by "significant plagiarism," according to turnitin.com, an online plagiarism-checking service.

But developing appropriate Internet skills goes far beyond preventing plagiarism—and needs to begin well before college.

Most experts say Internet research skills should be taught in middle school. Techno-savvy but naïve, nearly all middle school students today have been googling for years, according to Kathleen Schrock, a former librarian and technology administrator for Cape Cod's Nauset Public Schools and creator of "Kathy Schrock's Guide for Educators," an award-winning online compilation of curriculum-enhancement websites.

"Before grade six," says Schrock, "students don't have the knowledge base to do any serious Internet research." By middle school, she says, they are ready for their first introduction to advanced search techniques and Web resources.

Librarians, technology specialists, and classroom teachers who teach Web research skills say they focus on three main areas: how to search, how to evaluate, and how to avoid plagiarism through proper citation and attribution.

STARTING THE SEARCH

One of the first challenges for the novice researcher is how to begin. A few suggestions:

Wikipedia. Some teachers have students begin their research with a cursory glance at Wikipedia, the collaborative online encyclopedia. Although Wikipedia articles themselves cannot be considered reliable sources, since the content may change and the authorship is unknown, Schrock and others describe it as a terrific tool for gathering background information and particularly for finding links to useful, more conventional sources. Wikipedia's page on Pocahontas, for example, lists numerous books, links to more than a dozen websites, and citations for more than 20 other publications.

Wikipedia can also be valuable for its timeliness. When the former planet Pluto was demoted to "dwarf planet" status, for example, the "Pluto" entry on Wikipedia was updated within minutes, notes Cindi Phillip, president of the American Association for School Librarians.

Subscription-based online resources. Teachers also emphasize the importance of having students use library subscriptions to access periodicals online and search educational databases for additional information. Most school library media specialists have compiled extensive lists of gateway sites that offer links to a wide variety of online resources on specific topics or in subject areas that correspond to classroom curricula. Schrock's website lists many good gateway sites, such as *Best of History Web Sites*, sponsored by the Center for Teaching History with Technology, which provides sites appropriate for student research as well as lesson plans and classroom activities for teachers.

Key-word searches. Searching by key word on Google poses challenges for many students. Due to their lack of background knowledge, their word-association skills are limited. They may have trouble coming up with key words related to their topic, such as "teenage at-risk behavior" or "young alcoholics" for a topic on teen binge drinking.

Once they have created a list of key words, students need to learn how to limit their search to avoid having to sort through an avalanche of information. "I teach students to use the advanced search feature on Google [to the right of the search bar], which will allow them to hone their searches," says Schrock.

EVALUATING WEBSITES

Once students have begun a Google search, they often find it difficult to assess the quality of the hundreds of hits they may turn up, Schrock says. Some students look at the top three websites and think they're done, she says, while others mistakenly equate the most current site with the most reliable.

Librarian Phillip illustrates the problem of reliability to her students by showing them a PDF of a website called "Lake

Michigan Whale Watching" that presents purportedly scientific information about the whales and dolphins that live in Lake Michigan. Then she takes them to an encyclopedia or the National Geographic website—"sources kids know to have been checked for accuracy"—to show them that whales cannot live in fresh water. Through this exercise, Phillip teaches students to use multiple sources to check the information they gather.

She also shows them how to check websites to find out who is sponsoring the site or owns the material. Students whose Google search has landed them in the middle of a site should know how to look for its home page or use the URL, the top or bottom bars on the page, or the webmaster link to find clues to its sponsorship. The site name or links can then be googled for more information to detect any potential sources of bias and evaluate the site's credibility.

Students should also be encouraged to check the qualifications of people cited as experts by using Google, Who's Who, Wikipedia, or Amazon author searches, she says. A Web search for George Bell, the "marine biologist" cited on the Lake Michigan whale watching website, for example, comes up empty. Online subscription sources can also be used to research experts and verify facts found elsewhere.

All this searching and evaluating takes time, for teachers as well as students. Middle school teacher Garrison recommends that teachers budget as much time to help students with their research as they do to help with the writing itself.

AVOIDING PLAGIARISM

Plagiarism—the act of passing off another's words, ideas, images, work, or concepts as one's own—comes up every year in just about every classroom, teachers say, and the ease with which content can be copied and pasted off the Web has made it even more of a problem. "Kids don't always realize this is what they're doing, even after you've talked to them," says Garrison. "Sometimes they think that as long as they're citing the sources, they're OK."

Students ages 9 to 12 are ripe for learning about the ethics of attribution in research, says David Whittier, a Boston University education professor who has written about cyberethics. Whittier tells the story of a student who copies a file from the Internet and can't understand why that is "stealing" when the digital source "is still there" on the screen. Young students don't understand the concept of intellectual property, he explains, and may not grasp that material that is presented anonymously still has an author.

Many teachers warn students to use quotation marks and attributions every time they copy another's words. Brookline (Mass.) High School chemistry teacher Stephen Lantos, who assigns major research projects in all his classes, instructs students, "When in doubt, always cite." Noting that plagiarism sometimes occurs when students use jargon or borrow overly abstract terms or concepts, Lantos tells his students they may not use or even quote anything they don't understand. Instead, they must look up anything they don't know and restate what they have learned in their own words. Lantos also sets aside time to review student citations carefully.

To illustrate how easy it is to plagiarize unwittingly, some middle school teachers encourage students to run their work through online plagiarism checking services, such as turnitin.com, ithenticate.com, or canexus.com, before they turn their papers in. At the college level, these services can be used to enforce plagiarism policies. But when used independently by students, these services can be a useful—and eye-opening—tool.

Teachers can also structure research assignments in ways that will elicit original work. Topics that begin with "how" or "why" questions are usually more original and less vulnerable to plagiarism than fact-driven topics, teachers say. Lantos

THE FIVE Ws OF WEB RESEARCH

To help students assess the value of the sites they find, Web expert Kathleen Schrock suggests using the five *W*s as a rule of thumb:

- *Who* created the site? Can the authors be identified as experts?
- *What* is the author's purpose in creating the site?
- *When* was the site created or updated?
- *Where* does the information on the site come from?
- *Why* is the information useful to the student?

gives his students about 40 sample topics and then reviews project choices carefully with each student. He emphasizes the importance of allowing students to pick their topics as a way to own their material.

Garrison agrees that having a personal connection to the topic can encourage original thinking among students. She also passes out examples of previous student papers to illustrate good structure, research sources, citation references, and narrative voice. By making writing less daunting, she says, teachers can help students avoid falling into the trap of cut-and-paste plagiarism.

Although many schools have library or media specialists who can help students develop their Internet skills, they must still work closely with subject-area teachers. Brookline High's media specialist, Beverly Shinn, and her colleagues have developed an extensive curriculum that is distributed and reviewed every year in classrooms across the city. Nonetheless, she finds that such instruction is most effectively taught "at point of need," rather than in separate classes. Most students, she notes, "don't really learn the lessons until they've made the mistakes."

This chapter originally appeared in the September/October 2007 issue of the Harvard Education Letter.

FOR FURTHER INFORMATION

R. Beach. *teachingmedialiteracy.com: A Web-Linked Guide to Resources and Activities.* New York: Teachers College Press, 2007.

Best of History Web Sites. www.besthistorysites.net

"Kathy Schrock's Guide for Educators." school.discovery.com/schrockguide

J. Keane. *Internet-Based Student Research: Creating to Learn with a Step-by-Step Approach, Grades 5–12.* Worthington, OH: Linworth Publishing, 2006.

Lake Michigan Whale Watching. www.classroomhelp.com/lessons/web/WHALES/whale_in_MI.pdf

D. Whittier. "Cyberethics in the Googling Age." *Boston University School of Education Journal of Education* 187, no. 2 (2006): 1–77.

CHAPTER 2

Better Teaching with Web Tools

How blogs, wikis, and podcasts are changing the classroom

Colleen Gillard

- *Eric Langhorst's eighth-grade American History students in Liberty, Mo., listen to his podcasts about the Boston Tea Party while walking their dogs, doing chores, or getting ready for bed.*
- *Ben Sanoff's World History students in Berkeley, Calif., discuss their essays via instant messages before posting their final drafts to the class blog by midnight deadlines. Later they return to the blog to read and discuss one another's work.*
- *Fifth graders in College Park, Ga., create a wiki so compelling it receives over 1,000 hits from as far away as Indonesia, Turkey, and Latin America in the first few days after it's posted. The site, centered on a historical novel, includes a slide show, maps, historical background, and interviews.*

From blogs to wikis to podcasts, teachers in schools across the country are beginning to use Web tools to enhance student learning. If these tools are transforming how students learn, they're also changing how teachers teach.

Those who have waded into this brave new world say the use of Web tools in the classroom naturally propels teachers from lecturing at the front of the room to coaching from the back, a direction education professionals have been trying to steer teachers in for decades. With their peers—or the world—as their audience, students are eagerly seizing the opportunity to take charge of their learning.

This is what Debbie Herzig of Woodward Academy in College Park, Ga., says happened when she asked her fifth-grade students to build a wiki—a collaboratively written and edited website—around *Turn Homeward, Hannalee*, Patricia Beatty's book about Georgia mill workers during the Civil War. Students started the project with traditional classroom activities, like researching historical facts about the Civil War, creating a dictionary of mill terms, and taking a field trip to the ruins of a period mill. To create their wiki, students brainstormed topics for the website representing the important events and themes in the book, such as "Life of a Millworker" and "Civil War Timeline and Map." The students divided into groups to design and build these sections of the wiki, known as "wiki pages," and then critiqued one another's pages, editing for content, spelling, and grammar.

Students were motivated by the idea that their wiki could serve as a resource for other students and teachers on the Internet, according to Herzig. They were also enthusiastic about the opportunity to design their own wiki page and to edit one another's work. Herzig recalls that she and her coteacher had to resist the temptation to jump in and edit the students' work and learn to be comfortable with a "chaotic" process. Nonetheless, the teachers found the students patient and helpful with one another. "You always emphasize editing as an important part of the writing process, which can be a real chore for kids. But in this case, they really got its importance," says Herzig.

GETTING STARTED

Using Web tools comes more naturally to students than teachers, and young people will continue to outstrip adults in their use of these tools, says Will Richardson, a former teacher and author of the popular book, *Blogs, Wikis, Podcasts, and Other Powerful Web Tools for the Classroom.* "Kids instant message as if they were using a pencil. They use Facebook and My-Space without even thinking of them as blogs," he says.

For teachers, Web tools can seem fairly disruptive, not merely because they raise safety or privacy concerns, or even because of the technological challenges they present, "but more significantly because they demand a whole new pedagogical approach," says Richardson. "Information literacy should not be viewed as a technology curriculum separate from course curriculum, but more as a way to reconceive teaching and learning."

In fact, once teachers get the help they need to get started, many find that Web tools allow them to do the kinds of things they want to do in the classroom, such as promoting project-based learning, collaborative learning, and critical thinking (see "Examples of Classroom Blogs, Wikis, and Podcasts").

Fortunately, there are many resources available to help teachers experiment with Web-based projects (see "How to Get Started"). In planning her fifth graders' wiki, Herzig was assisted by the school's technology director, Shelley Paul, who claimed no real prior expertise other than reading Richardson's book. Wikis, whose name comes from the Hawaiian word *wiki-wiki* meaning "quick," involve installation on a server and are more complicated to set up than blogs, which can be created more easily on the Web through available websites. There are about "fifty flavors" of wiki software out there, Paul says. She did no programming, but simply downloaded free software onto her school's server. She also found short-and-sweet online instructions on how to format wiki text and

EXAMPLES OF CLASSROOM BLOGS, WIKIS, AND PODCASTS

Will Richardson's Modern American Literature blog on Sue Monk Kidd's *The Secret Lives of Bees* at Hunterdon Central Regional High School, Flemington, N.J.

weblogs.hcrhs.k12.nj.us/bees

Eric Langhorst's class blogs with embedded podcasts on Pat Hughes's *Guerilla Season* and Gary Blackwood's *The Year of the Hangman* at South Valley Junior High School, Liberty, Mo.

www.guerrillaseason.blogspot.com
www.theyearofthehangman.blogspot.com

Meriwether Lewis Elementary School wiki with podcasts and individual teacher "Classroom Notes" blogs, Portland, Ore.

www.lewiselementary.org

Debbie Herzig's fifth-grade wiki on *Look Homeward, Hannalee* at Woodward Academy, College Park, Ga.

woodward.edu/hannalee/doku.php?id=hannalee

Darren Kuropatwa's high school math blogs at Daniel McIntyre Collegiate Institute, Winnipeg, Canada.

Applied Math: **am40sw07.blogspot.com**
Pre-Calculus: **pc40sw07.blogspot.com**
AP Calculus: **apcalc06.blogspot.com**
For teachers: **adifference.blogspot.com**

Bob Sprankle's "Tech Time with Mr. S" podcasts at Wells Elementary School, Wells, Me.

weskids.com
For teachers: **www.bobsprankle.com**

HOW TO GET STARTED

Many websites provide opportunities for setting up blogs, wikis, and other nifty Web tools for educators. Many are free. For detailed help, see Will Richardson's website, **www.weblogg-ed .com**, or David Warlick's website, **www.landmark-project.com**.

Blogs (Web logs) are sequentially organized communication sites for exchanging information publicly or privately (within classrooms). Used as class portals, online filing cabinets for student work, or places for public conversations, blogs can include audio, video, and photo enhancements. See **www.blogger.com, edublogs.org, classwebs.net**, and **www.classblogmeister.com**. To search for blogs by keyword, visit **www.technorati.com**.

Wikis are content-management systems that encourage collaboration. Unlike blogs, wikis can be edited by participants. Such editing can be open (like Wikipedia's) or closed (class only). They demand some technical skill to install and are limited as text-editing tools, although some sites (called WYSIWYG, as in: What You See Is What You Get) offer editing interfaces closer to Word. See **www.writely.com, www.pbwiki.com**, or **seedwiki.com**.

Podcasts are basically amateur radio recordings, or audio files, created using built-in computer microphones. They are edited online and then downloaded to computers, blogs, wikis, or cell phones. See **audacity.sourceforge.net** or download Apple's iTunes software free at **www.apple.com/itunes** (Apple's podcast directory includes an education link).

Moodle is a free, easy-to-learn software package for educators. Installed on school servers, it features programs for creating tests, grades, forums, wikis, and blogs, and offers teachers oversight capabilities that allow them to see all a student's postings, coursework, or site visits. See **docs. moodle.org/en/About_Moodle**.

create links to other pages. Based on this information, Paul created a one-page cheat sheet for students, who were soon transcribing research, scanning photos, making art, and posting audio portions.

Beyond technical know-how, other hurdles to using Web tools in school often include safety and privacy concerns (see "Safety Advice"). For both blogs and wikis, many safety and security issues can be addressed through the choice of platform controlling access to the site. Most schools bar students from using full names, and many teachers vet all posts before they appear. Wikis have reversal buttons for restoring vandalized sites.

Ultimately, however, many believe that safety is not enforced so much by filters, which students can often defeat, as by education—like teaching audience awareness, how to recognize cyberbullying, and the rules of online etiquette.

SAFETY ADVICE

- Part of teachers' Web training must be about safety. Beyond reading the Children's Internet Protection Act (**www.fcc.gov/cgb/consumerfacts/cipa.html**), teachers should discuss school policies around student use of the Web.
- Remind students that they are posting as representatives of the school and that their language should reflect this. They need to remember that postings are public and may be permanent.
- Talk to students about cyberbullying and the importance of treating fellow students and other Web visitors with respect. Warn them that what they publish can be subject to disciplinary action, including lawsuits.

TAPPING THE "WOW" FACTOR

One blogging convert, Eric Langhorst, an eighth-grade teacher at South Valley Junior High in Liberty, Mo., has revamped his curriculum to include Web tools. With his students, Langhorst built a book blog—or online journal—around Pat Hughes's novel *Guerrilla Season*, which details the atrocities committed by Missouri neighbors during the Civil War. Langhorst posted questions to draw out students' opinions on what they were reading and help students make connections to current events like the war in Iraq. Students were required to submit comments to the blog anonymously or with first names only. The book's author also participated in the blog, responding to student questions and uploading podcasts on her research, which students could listen to on their computers or iPods.

In addition to motivating students by tapping into the "wow" factor, Langhorst says blogging gives them the chance to get more involved and spend more quality time on a project, since they can work where and when they want. "They can participate in the blog at home, in the library, etc., instead of limiting their educational experience to just a 45-minute class that takes place in one location," he says.

Another benefit of the blog project was a noticeable increase in family involvement. "The biggest change I saw was that some of the students shared the experience of reading the novel and using the blog with their family," Langhorst says. "In one case, a student told me that she read the novel with her dad and then they both went online to read comments from the author and leave a comment. When was the last time you heard of a father and daughter reading a novel together and asking the author questions that had immediate feedback?"

A NATURAL FORUM FOR TEENS

Berkeley (Calif.) High School history teacher Ben Sanoff uses both blogs and wikis to hold online discussions for his classes. Students also submit essays—with their names removed—for peer editing. Blogs are a natural forum for teens, "who prefer to talk to their peers," he says. "You wouldn't believe how often they check the site for responses to their posts."

On the nights he requires online discussions on particular issues, Sanoff says, the students "work hard not to embarrass themselves. They want to sound smart and coherent." Because the blog gives students more time and space to organize their thoughts, he believes it gives them better opportunities to learn and model how to build logical arguments, which is especially helpful for the weaker students.

Students using the blog also get more feedback on their writing than he can provide as an individual teacher. "I have 120 students spread between five classes and can't possibly give everyone the attention they need. So I throw up a grading rubric, have them post their essays, and then comment on each other's work," he says.

Sanoff says he's never had a problem with cyberbullying because his students know that he's monitoring the classroom site. Nor does the so-called digital divide seem to be a problem. Even students without home computers participate, he says. "They seem to manage somehow, whether at a library or with friends. I worried about this before realizing that nearly all kids are accessing MySpace or Facebook or e-mail or something anyway all the time."

THE NEW DIGITAL DIVIDE

Teaching students to use computers creatively and collaboratively is exactly what is needed, many experts say, to bridge what they see as a new digital divide. "The digital divide no longer defines those with or without a computer," explains Tim Magner, director of the office of educational technology at the U.S. Department of Education (DOE). "Increasingly, it has more to do with degrees of Web facility." Having access to a computer, he explains, does not mean that a person can easily navigate the glut of information now available on the Web to produce something new and useful. "Operational facility is less an end goal than a way to get to critical thinking, innovation, and invention," he says.

Indeed, the very definition of literacy must expand to include the ability to effectively research, converse, and publish through the Web, argues David F. Warlick, a former teacher and author of *Classroom Blogging: A Teacher's Guide to the Blogosphere*. "We're spending too much time teaching students about paper," he says. Citing a study by the School of Information Management and Systems at the University of California at Berkeley, Warlick points to the five "exabytes" of new information produced in 2002—enough for 37,000 more libraries the size of the Library of Congress. Of that, only .01 percent has actually been published in print. With the right skills, Warlick says, teachers can show students how to mine this expanding lode of information to create "personal digital libraries" that are far richer and more timely than any printed book.

"How to identify the specific skill set students will need in the 21st century to be computer literate—this discussion will evolve as the technology grows and changes," the DOE's Magner says. But one thing is clear, he adds: "Students need greater sophistication in using these information and communication Web tools if they wish to engage in what is becoming an increasingly complex future."

For more information on web tools see "Top 10 Web Tools for Teachers."

TOP 10 WEB TOOLS FOR TEACHERS

By Dave Saltman

In the quest to work smarter, not harder, teachers are flocking to an ever-expanding galaxy of web-based tools for help with everything from classroom management to classroom discussions. Here are some tools that are now grabbing teachers' attention—and the attention of their students. Virtually all are free, with a few offering paid upgrades that add some technological bling.

Managing for Efficiency

Education's not-so-little secret is the enormity of the management task. Addressing this reality, many teachers have set up class websites using purveyors like Google Sites (www.google.com/sites) and Weebly (http://education.weebly.com) to provide a place to post assignments, class documents, and announcements. And why not? They're free and easy to create. Now, Edmodo (www.edmodo.com) is getting kudos as an all-in-one organizational solution with its simple Facebook-like interface. It provides teachers with a central place to present assignments and associated materials, grade student work, and communicate with students (as a class or privately), while also offering them a place to upload work and communicate with peers.

"What I like about Edmodo is the ability to have all classes in one location, as well as being able to break them down into smaller groups," notes Jodi Tompkins, a technology specialist in the Eldon, Mo., school district.

However, Edmodo has not supplanted wikis—hyperlinked web pages that anyone can edit. Wikipedia is based on this technology and some teachers first jumped to the web by creating hyperlinked class web pages using the free version of Wikispaces (www.wikispaces.com). Many teachers are using both Edmodo and wikis. Fern Vogt, a Siloam Springs, Ark., technology coordinator and teacher says foreign language teachers have used Edmodo in her school district to accept .mp3 files of students' pronunciation and usage recordings. Vogt sets up wikis, too, for elementary students to edit their own pages, depending upon assignment needs. Wikis also offer a convenient place for students to post links to components of their ongoing projects or portfolios, Vogt says.

Enriching Communication

The social aspect of school is undeniable; leveraging this reality occupies legions of educators and programmers. A number of tools support so-called back-channel classroom activities on the Internet: real-time communication among students and between students and the teacher while a whole-class activity—a movie or a science demonstration, for example—is occurring.

Richard Byrne, a history teacher at Oxford Hills Comprehensive High School in South Paris, Maine, who also authors the blog *Free Technology for Teachers* (www.freetech4teachers.com), sets up a forum using Chatzy (www.chatzy.com) or TodaysMeet (http://todaysmeet.com) to let students converse in real time while they are taking in a presentation or watching a documentary. Using their laptops, students may freely discuss the presentation, but Byrne monitors the chat from his screen to make sure it stays on topic. "It's great for kids that need a lot of clarification," Byrne says, "or kids that take in things through conversation."

Some teachers are pursuing back-channel activities using cell phones, once they obtain permission to use the texting features

continued

or Twitter for activities. The web is replete with Twitter-based lessons. Byrne adds that Edmodo's micro-blogging feature supports this kind of activity as well.

New applications such as Vocaroo (http://vocaroo.com) and Voki (www.voki.com) enable students to record voice messages and send them to the web. The latter also enables the creation of speaking avatars, which teachers and students can embed in blogs to, for example, introduce a topic on a wiki or present a book review.

What do kids learn from these lessons? All these new communication tools can help reinforce and measure student understanding by giving students multiple ways to present what they have learned in their own ways. To gauge student comprehension, or get student opinions on a range of topics, teachers can also set up online polls with Poll Everywhere (www.polleverywhere.com).

This article originally appeared in the March/April 2011 issue of the *Harvard Education Letter.*

This chapter originally appeared in the May/June 2007 issue of the Harvard Education Letter.

FOR FURTHER INFORMATION

How Much Information? 2003. Available online at http://www2.sims.berkeley.edu/research/projects/how-much-info-2003/execsum.htm

W. Richardson. *Blogs, Wikis, Podcasts, and Other Powerful Web Tools for the Classroom.* Thousand Oaks, CA: Corwin Press, 2006.

D.R. Warlick. *Classroom Blogging: A Teacher's Guide to the Blogosphere*. Raleigh, NC. The Landmark Project, 2005. Available at landmarkproject.com

N.E. Willard. *Cyberbullying and Cyberthreats: Responding to the Challenge of Online Social Aggression, Threats, and Distress.* Champaign, IL: Research Press, 2007.

CHAPTER 3

"Dumb" Phones, Smart Lessons

Schools answer student calls for mobile computing

Colleen Gillard

In Santa Ana, Calif., Judy Pederson smiles when she sees her ninth-grade English Literature class bent over their cell phones, furiously texting. They are engaged and on task, and she will soon have their thoughts on the possible consequences of Friar Lawrence marrying two star-crossed lovers in 16th-century Verona. The students' texts go from their phones to a website to the white board on her classroom wall.

"Before, it was difficult getting them to write," says the Valley High School teacher, who has decided to exploit rather than fight the oft-observed teen addiction to cell phones. "But now when I ask them to compose back stories or give advice to conflicted literary characters, they're into it." Her only requirement is that her students, who generally come from first-generation immigrant homes, use standard English.

Only four years ago, 19 percent of computing devices in K–12 schools were mobile devices, according to the report America's Digital Schools 2006. That number has increased to 57 percent, according to a national survey of nearly 1,000 school principals and technology coordinators to be released in September by the research group Project RED. Cell phone ownership among students has increased as well. According to a 2010 Kaiser Family Foundation study, 85 percent of high school students, 69 percent of middle school students, and 31 percent of eight- to ten-year-olds now own cell phones.

SEIZING ON WHAT KIDS HAVE

For educators concerned with the digital divide, or with their districts' ability to afford technology upgrades, the popularity of cell phones among students has come as an unexpected resource arriving in their classroom. "The beauty of cell phones is that you don't need a certain demographic; all kids have them," says Liz Kolb, a University of Michigan education instructor, who wrote the 2008 book *Toys to Tools: Connecting Student Cell Phones to Education*. Kolb is a proponent of teaching with the plainest tech device in mind. "You focus on what [most] kids have at the moment," she says.

When Pederson discovered that many of her students did not have computers or Internet access at home, and yet 88 percent had cell phones, she realized she was onto something. Having her students use their phones for in-class activities meant simply organizing them in groups to cover those without, and ensuring that homework assignments included technology-free options.

She focused her lessons around the capabilities of the dumbest phone—not too great a handicap since even the plainest phones could access websites through simple calls or texts, and download podcasts or other content. Blog sites have also made such actions as the posting of texts or recorded material onto class or individual blogs easy (see "Using 'Dumb' Phones in School").

A TOOL FOR TEACHERS, TOO

Teachers, in turn, are finding that having students text answers to questions via websites allows them an on-the-spot

USING "DUMB" PHONES IN SCHOOL

According to Liz Kolb, author of *Toys to Tools: Connecting Student Cell Phones to Education*, there are many ways teachers can use even the simplest cell phones—those that can send text, photos, and recorded audio to websites.

Here are some suggested cell-phone activities by subject:

- *Science*: Students can use their phones in a treasure-hunt exercise to photograph and post their descriptions and identifications of objects of scientific interest like rocks, plants or insects. These pictures, along with text, can be sent in a message from their cell phone to go@blogger.com. No prior Blogger account is necessary; the message itself is sufficient to create the new blog.
- *History*: Using this same method, students go on field trips to take pictures of and record text about historical landmarks, people interviewed, or other relevant items to post to their blog.
- *Geography*: Students can take pictures of different geographical places and send the photos to a class Flickr account.
- *Foreign Languages*: Besides listening to foreign-language podcasts on their phones, students can create short telenovelas (Spanish-language soap operas) using the camcorders on their phones to record and post to their blog.
- *Literature*: Twitter can be used as a forum for posting quick thoughts, questions, or reactions to a class reading or assignment. Students can also collaborate on writing stories, called "twittories," by tweeting successive entries. Students can practice class presentations as well as participate in poetry slams by recording themselves on their cell phones and posting to a class website.

gauge of student understanding. For such quick assessments, many teachers use the free Web tool www.polleverywhere .com to get instant feedback from short multiple-choice tests as well as from responses to more open-ended questions. The website enables teachers to post or graph student answers on electronic whiteboards in real time—fast results that both students and teachers like.

Jimbo Lamb, who teaches math at Annville-Cleona High School in rural, central Pennsylvania, uses www.polleverywhere .com to let him know when to move on to the next lesson. "With many students too shy to admit what they don't understand, it's always difficult to get a clear sense how a lesson is going. But with a tool that enables student anonymity, I get a quick and accurate picture."

Making use of cell phones in the classroom—rather than banning them—creates an opportunity to structure their use in a positive way, and to talk about cyberbullying and other inappropriate uses of the technology, teachers say. Judy Pederson believes that having students help compose classroom rules for cell phone use encourages compliance. In her classroom, cell phones that aren't put away when not being used are confiscated until a parent can come to retrieve them. Kolb advises teachers to ask students to leave their cell phones at the front of the room until needed for classroom activities.

SMART PHONES MAY BE NEXT

Meanwhile, pressure to expand cell phone use in the classroom continues to come from the kids. After New Milford (NJ) High School principal Eric Sheninger bought his staff an iPod cart with 28 iPods and an iMac computer for downloading curriculum-enrichment materials from the Web—he was chagrined to hear from students that they would have preferred smart phones instead. Smart phones comprise only two percent of mobile devices used in schools, according to the Project RED survey, but their presence is projected to increase in the near future. Since smart phones require Internet data plans, which currently cost around 30 dollars a month per phone (in addition to flat usage fees), they represent a sustained investment few schools can afford.

Nonetheless teens keep asking—something Shawn Gross, managing director of Digital Millennial Consulting, learned in 2006 when his educational-technology advisory group teamed up with the U.S. Department of Education to survey 300 disengaged students in the Washington, DC, metro area about how technology could improve the teenagers' interest in and understanding of math and science. Students told researchers that they learned best when collaborating with peers and, when asked to name their choice of technological learning tools, overwhelmingly chose smart phones over fancy new laptops. Students complained about the "hassle" posed by laptops: having to retrieve them from backpacks, finding somewhere to open them, and then waiting as they boot up. "Teenagers today want instant and continuous access to the Web," Gross says.

The research team heard, but wanted to see if such complaints held up across socioeconomic and regional differences. Gross partnered with an educational nonprofit, Project Tomorrow, to ask a national sample of 350,000 students for their learning-tool preference. They received the same response: a clear majority favored smart phones over any other technology, including laptops. "The critical factors for these kids seemed to be instant, continuous access to the Internet; easy, immediate access to the device; and quick, simple contact with their peers," Gross says.

For the time being, not a lot of schools are pursuing the smart-phone route unless it is with outside funding. But over time, if fees come down, Gross notes, schools may be seeing more and more students show up in class with parent-financed devices.

This chapter originally appeared in the July/August 2010 issue of the Harvard Education Letter.

CHAPTER 4

Teaching 21st Century Skills

What does it look like in practice?

Nancy Walser

Call it a quiet revolution. As 2014 approaches—the deadline for all students to be proficient on state tests—academics, educators, business groups, and policymakers are finding common ground in a movement to bring "21st century skills" to the classroom, prompting state agencies and district leaders across the country to rewrite curriculum standards and even to contemplate big changes to existing state testing systems.

What are 21st century skills, who's pushing them, and what does 21st century teaching look like in practice?

Although definitions vary, most lists of 21st century skills include those needed to make the best use of rapidly changing technologies; the so-called "soft skills" that computers can't provide, like creativity; and those considered vital to working and living in an increasingly complex, rapidly changing global society (see "Skills for a New Century").

"Some of these skills have always been important but are now taking on another meaning—like collaboration. Now you have to be able to collaborate across the globe with someone

SKILLS FOR A NEW CENTURY

Most lists of 21st century skills include some or all of the following:

- Critical thinking
- Problem-solving
- Collaboration
- Written and oral communication
- Creativity
- Self-direction
- Leadership
- Adaptability
- Responsibility
- Global awareness

you might never meet," explains Christopher Dede, a Harvard professor who sits on the Massachusetts 21st Century Skills Task Force. "Some are unique to the 21st century. It's only relatively recently, for example, that you could get two million hits on an [Internet] search and have to filter down to five that you want."

While progressive educators in the past have often been wary of education reforms spearheaded by big business, the outsourcing of menial jobs and the need for workers to compete in a global economy have brought about an unprecedented convergence of interests, argues Tony Wagner, author of *The Global Achievement Gap* and codirector of Harvard University's Change Leadership Group. Surveys of business leaders show that when hiring new employees, they are looking for the same higher-order thinking skills as those considered necessary for students to do well in college, he notes.

Wagner and others also point to signs of student disengagement from traditional forms of learning that value memorization and mastery of content over student-designed demonstrations of skills. They cite surveys indicating that U.S. high schoolers drop out more from boredom than failure.

"Making AYP [adequate yearly progress] is absolutely no guarantee that students will be ready for college, citizenship, and employment," says Wagner, noting the high number of students needing remedial coursework in college—including those who graduate from schools boasting high standardized test scores. "Our curriculum is information-based and the emphasis is to acquire information first and foremost, and secondarily acquire skills," he says. "We have it exactly backwards."

Teaching 21st century skills doesn't necessarily mean using a lot of technology, although projects may involve computers, software, and other devices, like a global positioning system (GPS). Sometimes it's simply a matter of approaching an assignment differently to allow students to demonstrate skills like teamwork, collaboration, and self-directed learning. Equally important is making sure teachers are able to coach students on how to advance to the next level of a particular skill. This is often done with rubrics that explain clearly what poor, average, and effective skills look like in practice.

What follows are some examples of 21st century teaching provided by researchers, curriculum specialists, administrators, and teachers.

Try a Socratic seminar. Instead of relying on the usual lecture-question format, ninth-grade humanities teachers Mark Rubin-Toles and Torie Leinbach, who teach in the Catalina Foothills school district outside Tucson, Ariz., require students to lead their own discussions about a book, documentary, or document they have studied. Students are graded on the quality of their participation. Good marks go to those who build on, clarify, or challenge others' comments while referencing information from the material, their own experience, or other current events, according to a rubric given to them in advance.

"In the beginning, they struggle a lot," says Rubin-Toles, who limits his role to mapping the interactions on paper while the students talk. "There are these long silences and the kids are very uncomfortable." Later in the year, in the best of conversations, the students make connections with material they discussed earlier, he says.

The exercise builds critical thinking, oral communication, flexibility, self-direction, and teamwork. "They have to listen to others to do well," says Rubin-Toles. "Part of teamwork is holding back, especially when you have something to say. It's like a meeting of adults."

Beautify the neighborhood. Sixth-grade science teacher Wayne Naylor has found a way to weave 21st century skills into lessons on longitude and latitude and on scale and proportion—required by Indiana state standards—while also working to get his town certified as a wildlife community by the National Wildlife Federation. In his class at Craig Middle School, students work in groups to identify natural areas in surrounding Lawrence Township that need improvement. One such project was restoring and renovating the city's Fall Creek Park to remove invasive species. Using the Internet, students researched plants native to the area. They conducted surveys to gather ideas from others in the community about their plans. Using a GPS and Google Earth, they marked the locations of their projects and created poster displays and scale models. Some groups went further, producing a videotape to apply for a national Christopher Columbus award, which is given to teams of middle school students who use science and technology to find an innovative solution to a community problem. The students are in the process of implementing the plans they designed.

Naylor's six-week unit has something to engage everyone, he says. One student with attendance problems never missed Naylor's class. Although the student struggled in math class, when it came to translating proportions from a model picnic table to build the real thing (which now sits in the school courtyard), "he did just fine," says Naylor. "He was a leader. Everyone was really impressed."

Build a bridge. Not everyone has access to 40-foot pine trees, but in rural Darlington, Wisc., high school teacher Dick Anderson seized the opportunity to use local rough-sawn timber to impart some 21st century skills and real-world entrepreneurship to his students.

Each year for the past two years, students in Anderson's elective Building Trades class have been involved with nearly every aspect of planning, budgeting, modeling, building, and siting a rustic covered bridge. Students worked 60 hours outside of school to complete the last one. In a real lesson in adaptability, the plan to site it over the nearby Pecatonica River had to be abandoned due to environmental issues. The plans were scaled down so the bridge would fit in a city park near a new motel.

The project went beyond the typical trades class in which students learn technical skills in isolation from the real world, says Anderson. Students gave numerous presentations to school board members, the city council, and business groups, and even gave interviews to reporters from a local TV station. "They had to convince responsible adults to say, 'Yes, we'll take a bridge for the city of Darlington,'" said Anderson. "They learned that if you want to get anything done, that's the way it is."

Make an I-Movie. Catalina Foothills teacher Dana Mulay and her kindergarten class were getting bored with point-and-click software games. So, to keep her five-year-olds excited about learning, she decided to help them use I-Movies software to create videos featuring the solid shapes they were studying in math. She divided them into teams and, armed with digital cameras, they went into the desert nearby hunting for shapes to photograph. "Barrel cactus sort of look like spheres and a seguero [cactus] is a cylinder," she says. She downloaded the photos onto laptops brought into the class on carts, and students worked in pairs to make the movies, using invented spelling for captions. The project helped them learn more not only about computers, but also about teamwork and self-direction, she says. "It was really amazing to see them problem-solve on their own and focus on what they needed to do."

Save a river. A block and a half away from the seventh most endangered river in the United States sits the Hayes Bilingual Elementary School in Milwaukee. It's where library media specialist Tomas Kelnhofer is using 21st century tools to work with fifth-grade teachers and students—the majority of whom come from Spanish-speaking homes—to learn about science, their community, and their planet. The Kinnickinnic River "has been an eyesore—a drainage ditch and dumping ground," says Kelnhofer. Except for occasional debris floating down the wide, concrete-lined channel, the river was invisible to students. Not anymore. Partnering with local health and environmental groups, students have canoed down the river to see places where PCB-laden sediment has collected. They have tested water for bacteria, posted reflections in online journals using Moodle, and created a DVD and PowerPoint presentations of their plans to enhance the river area. They have also debated moral dilemmas such as whether the city of Milwaukee should continue to use salt on icy roads for safety, given the impact on wildlife in the river. "It's true that our students are going through a continuous revolving door of assessments, including those required by NCLB," says Kelnhofer. "However, in between these assessment cycles there is time to work on research and projects that focus both on content and process skills."

STANDARDS AND ASSESSMENT

The possibilities for infusing 21st century skills into classrooms are "endless," maintains Ken Kay, president of the Partnership for 21st Century Skills, an advocacy organization that works with states. Yet there is far more agreement on how these skills can be taught than on how to encourage teachers to teach them in the current climate of high-stakes testing (see "Leaders in 21st Century Learning"). Existing curricula are driven largely by the statewide assessments mandated by the No Child Left Behind Act. Simply adding new standards for 21st century skills to existing ones isn't realistic, experts say, since most state standards pack in "27 years' worth of content" for teachers to cover in 12 years, as Dede puts it. Some things will have to go or be "de-emphasized," he says. "There is absolutely no reason to teach state capitals any more, because you can look it up in 15 seconds on a computer and because it's not foundational to learning anything else."

Another knotty issue is assessment. Typical multiple-choice tests can't be used to measure things like teamwork. Newer tests designed to assess critical thinking or problem-solving skills, like the Program for International Student Assessment (PISA), are only recently being piloted in a few U.S. districts. Efforts to implement performance assessments, like those being pursued by a consortium of 28 high schools in New York State as an alternative to high-stakes tests, are also rare.

The Partnership for 21st Century Skills advocates a blend of old and new. "Ultimately, we view this as the future of the No Child Left Behind Act, which measures whether students can perform core skills," says Kay. "The real issue is, do we have the collective will to make 21st century skills a priority?"

LEADERS IN 21ST CENTURY LEARNING

Some states and districts are forging ahead with revising curricula and tests to incorporate 21st century skills, however they define them.

- North Carolina, the first state to join the Partnership for 21st Century Skills, has adopted a mission statement and goals for teaching 21st century skills and is completing new standards for students, teachers, principals, and superintendents. Every middle school will have digital literacy coaches and every high school will have a digital learning advisor.
- West Virginia, another Partnership member, has rewritten its statewide standards and will give the first of its revised state tests next May. The state has also invested heavily in professional development, establishing two different institutes for principals and teachers and a Teach21 website.
- Wisconsin is in the midst of revising its math and English curriculum with an eye to incorporating 21st century skills. One example of a change: new language in the math standards might stipulate that students will be able to apply probability and statistics to understand an economic, social, or environmental issue. "Learning content in isolation doesn't stick," says Paul Sandrock, assistant director of the content and learning team for the Wisconsin Department of Public Instruction.
- In Iowa, which joined the Partnership in March, the state department of education is developing model units to help teachers embed 21st century skills into the curriculum and beginning to look at how and whether to assess them. "Assessment of 21st century skills must go beyond [current] multiple-choice standardized assessments," says department director Judy Jeffrey.

- In Arizona, the Catalina Foothills district settled on 12 skills to teach their students and has rewritten its standards and report cards with those in mind.
- The Virginia Beach, Va., school district has just completed a yearlong strategic planning process that included 250 community members. "The resounding message was, 'Forget the tests, don't worry about the scores, prepare our kids for the world,'" says superintendent James Merrill. As a result, the 72,000-student district is looking at only one strategic goal for the next five years: "By 2015, students will master the skills they need to succeed to be 21st century learners, workers, and citizens."

Others, like Dede, believe that until states adopt better ways to measure 21st century skills, it will be difficult to bring about a shift in classroom priorities.

"You can't just sprinkle 21st century skills on the 20th century doughnut," he says. "It requires a fundamental reconception of what we're doing."

This chapter originally appeared in the September/October 2008 issue of the Harvard Education Letter.

FOR FURTHER INFORMATION

Catalina Foothills School District: www.cfsd16.org

Christopher Columbus Awards: www.christophercolumbusawards.com

Darlington, Wisc. High School Timber Framed Covered Bridge Project: www.summerville-novascotia.com/darlingtoncoveredbridge/

C. Dede. *Transforming Education for the 21st Century: New Pedagogies That Help All Students Attain Sophisticated Learning Outcomes.* Available online at www.gse.harvard.edu/~dedech/Dede_21stC-skills_semi-final.pdf

Iowa Core Curriculum and 21st Century Skills: www.iowa.gov/educate/content/view/674/1023

F. Levy and R. Murnane. *The New Division of Labor: How Computers are Creating the Next Job Market*. Princeton, NJ: Princeton University Press, 2005.

The New York Performance Standards Consortium: http://performanceassessment.org

North Carolina Professional Teaching Standards: www.ncptsc.org

Partnership for 21st Century Skills: www.21stcenturyskills.org

T. Wagner. *The Global Achievement Gap*. New York: Basic Books, 2008.

West Virginia Department of Education Teach21: http://wvde.state.wv.us/teach21

Wisconsin 21st Century Skills Initative: www.21stcenturyskills.org/route21/

CHAPTER 5

The Classroom of Popular Culture

**What video games can teach us about
making students *want* to learn**

James Paul Gee

Why is it that many children can't sit still long enough to finish their homework and yet will spend hours playing games on the computer? Video games are spectacularly successful at engaging young learners. It's not because they are easy. Good video games are long, complex, and difficult. They have to be; if they were dumbed down, no one would want to play. But if children couldn't figure out how to play them—and have fun doing so—game designers would soon go out of business.

To succeed, game designers incorporate principles of learning that are well supported by current research. Put simply, they recruit learning as a form of pleasure. Games like *Rise of Nations*, *Age of Mythology*, *Deus Ex*, *The Elder Scrolls III: Morrowind*, and *Tony Hawk's Underground* teach children not only how to play but how to learn, and to keep on learning.

Children have to learn long, complex, and difficult things in school, too. They need to be able to learn in deep ways: to improvise, innovate, and challenge themselves; to develop concepts, skills, and relationships that will allow them to

47

explore new worlds, to experience learning as a source of enjoyment and as a way to explore and discover who they are. Let's look at how this kind of learning works in cutting-edge video games. We might learn something ourselves.

PRODUCERS, NOT CONSUMERS

To start with, good video games offer players strong identities. In some games, players learn to view the virtual world through the eyes of a distinctive personality, like the solitary Special Forces operative Solid Snake in the espionage action game *Metal Gear Solid*. In others, like the epic role-playing game *The Elder Scrolls III: Morrowind*, each player builds a character from the ground up and explores the game from that character's point of view. Game designers recognize that learning and identity are interrelated. Learning a new domain, whether physics or furniture-making, requires students to see the world in new ways—in the ways physicists or furniture-makers do.

Game designers let players be producers, not just consumers. Players codesign a game through their unique actions and decisions. Many games come with software that allows players to modify ("mod") them to produce new scenarios or whole new games. For instance, in the *Tony Hawk* skateboarding games, players can design their own skate parks. At another level, an open-ended game like *The Elder Scrolls III: Morrowind*, in which each character undertakes his or her own journey, ultimately becomes a different experience for each player.

Players can also customize games to fit their learning and playing styles, since well-designed games allow problems to be solved in multiple ways. For example, in the two *Deus Ex* games, many of the problems a player faces can be solved in at least three ways: using stealth, confrontation, or persuasion. Many games also offer levels of play for beginning, experienced, or advanced players, letting players choose the degree of challenge they are comfortable with. In some games, players can test their own skills. For example, the real-time strategy game *Rise of Nations* asks, "How fast can you get to the Gunpowder Age? Find out if your resource-management skills are good enough."

Features like these encourage players to take risks, explore, and try new things. If they fail, the consequences are minimal—they can start over from their last saved game. All these factors give players a real sense of agency, ownership, and control. It's *their* game.

A CYCLE OF MASTERY

But learning goes yet deeper in well-designed games. Research has shown that when learners are left completely free to solve a complex problem, they may hit on creative solutions. But these solutions may not necessarily help them generate good hypotheses for solving later problems, even easier ones. A simple classroom example is the case of the young child who comes to think that reading means memorizing words. This may work perfectly well—until the child is swamped by the marked increase in vocabulary in more complex books.

In good video games problems are well ordered, so that early ones lead the player to formulate hypotheses that work well for solving later, harder problems. For example, if stealth is important in a game, the first levels will clearly show the player why confrontation is a less effective option, so as not to reinforce skills that will later undermine the player's success.

This well-ordered sequence creates an ongoing cycle of consolidation and challenge that enables players to confront an initial set of problems, and then practice solving them until they have routinized their mastery. The game then throws out a new class of problem, requiring players to come up with new solutions. This phase of mastery is consolidated through repetition, only to be challenged again. In this way, good

THE RULES OF THE GAME

Challenging, fun, well-designed video games incorporate important principles of learning that are solidly supported by recent research. Why can't we base our classroom instruction on the same rules?

- Create motivation for extended learning.
- Create and honor preparation for future learning.
- Create and honor "horizontal" learning experiences—letting learners try out and consolidate their skills in different contexts at the same level, rather than hurrying them from one level to the next.
- Let learners assess their own previous knowledge and learning styles.
- Build in choices from the beginning.
- Banish the word "remedial."
- Teach skills in a simplified context so learners can see how the skills fit together and how to apply them.

games stay within, but at the outer edge of, the player's competence. They feel doable, but challenging. This makes them pleasantly frustrating, putting players in what psychologists call a "flow" state.

Video games operate on the principle of "performance before competence." That is, players can learn as they play, rather than having to master an entire body of knowledge before being able to put it to use. Research shows that students learn best when they learn in context—that is, when they can relate words, concepts, skills, or strategies to prior experience. In fact, many students are alienated from what they learn in school because those connections and experiences are

- Give information in multiple modes at once (print, visual, oral).
- Provide information "just in time" and "on demand."
- Let learners customize what you are offering.
- Minimize the distinction between learning and playing. Use developmental (not evaluative) tests that allow learners to discover the outer edge of their competence and help them operate just inside that edge.
- Allow learners to practice their skills, and then challenge them to develop new ones. Repeat.
- Ensure that learners at every level have access to knowledge that is distributed and dispersed among people, places, sites, texts, tools, and technologies
- Create an affinity space where learners can interact with peers and masters around a shared interest.

Adapted from *Situated Language and Learning*, by James Paul Gee (New York: Routledge, 2004).

absent. Video games are simulations of new experiences and new worlds, yet they are able to engage players with languages and ways of thinking with which they have no prior experience. Players encounter new words and techniques in the context of play, not as abstract definitions or sets of rules. This holds their interest and spurs them on to develop new skills, vocabularies, relationships, and attitudes—irrespective of factors like race and class.

One way players can increase their competence is to seek advice from other players. There are websites and Internet chat rooms for almost any game, where players trade tips and stories, and where questions can be posted. Experts can help novices and peers can pool information. New knowledge is available just in time—when players need it—or on demand—when players ask for it.

PREPARATION FOR A COMPLEX WORLD

Finally, good video games nurture higher-order thinking skills. They encourage players to think in terms of relationships, not isolated events or facts. In a game like *Rise of Nations*, for example, players need to think about how each step they take might affect their future actions and the actions of their opponents as they try to advance their civilizations through the ages. These kinds of games encourage players to explore their options thoroughly rather than taking the straightest and swiftest path, and to reconceive their goals from time to time—good skills in a world full of complex, high-risk systems.

Video games teach players to capitalize on "smart tools," distributed knowledge, and cross-functional teams. The virtual characters one manipulates in a game are smart tools. They have skills and knowledge of their own, which they lend to the player. For example, the citizens in *Rise of Nations* know how to build cities, but the player needs to know where to build them. In multiplayer games like *World of WarCraft*, players form teams in which each player contributes a different set of skills. Each player must master a specialty, since a Mage plays differently than a Warrior, but the players must understand each other's specializations well enough to coordinate with one another. Thus, the knowledge needed to play the games is distributed among a set of real people and their smart tools, much as in a modern science lab or high-tech workplace.

In his bestselling book *The World Is Flat*, Thomas Friedman argues that the United States is facing a looming educational crisis. Even highly skilled jobs in radiology, computer science, or engineering are being outsourced to low-cost cen-

PLAYING WITH WORDS

One of the biggest predictors of success in school is the size of a child's vocabulary. Many children struggle to master the specialized language used in math, social studies, or science. But look at this typical description of a Bulbasaur, one of the Pokémon characters, from the game's trading card:

> Bulbasaur are a combination of Grass-type and Poison-type Pokémon. Because they are Grass-type Pokémon, Bulbasaur have plantlike characteristics such as the large, leafy growth on their back. Over time, Bulbasaur will evolve into Ivysaur and Venusaur.

There are lots of low-frequency words here, and complex syntax as well. The content is also challenging: There are 150 Pokémon characters, categorized into roughly 16 types. Each has a specialized set of skills, and many can evolve into one or two other characters. Yet children as young as six master the language and rules of Pokémon, and there is no evidence that socioeconomic factors have any impact on their skill or interest in the game.

ters. Any job that involves standardized skills can be exported. To maintain their competitive advantage, workers in industrialized countries will need to go beyond a mastery of standardized skills to become flexible, adaptive, lifelong learners of new skills. Yet U.S. schools are focused more than ever on the "basics," measuring their success with standardized tests that assess standardized skills.

It is ironic that young people today are often exposed to more creative and challenging learning experiences in popular culture than they are in school. The principles on which video-game design is based are foundational to the kind of learning that enables children to become innovators and life-long learners. Yet how many of today's classrooms actually incorporate these principles as thoroughly and deeply as these games do? Let's ask ourselves how we can make learning in or out of school more "game-like"—not in the sense of playing games in class, but by making the experience of learning as motivating, stimulating, collaborative, and rewarding as the experience of playing a well-designed video game.

This chapter originally appeared in the November/December 2005 issue of the Harvard Education Letter.

FOR FURTHER INFORMATION

J.C. Beck and M. Wade. *Got Game: How the Gamer Generation Is Reshaping Business Forever.* Boston: Harvard Business School Press, 2005.

J.P. Gee. *What Video Games Have to Teach Us about Learning and Literacy.* New York: Palgrave/Macmillian, 2003.

R. Koster. *Theory of Fun for Game Design.* Phoenix: Paraglyph, 2004.

Go to www.academiccolab.org/initiatives/gapps.html for many other papers related to games and learning.

PART II

Technology and Assessment

CHAPTER 6

Online Testing, Version 1.0

Oregon's adaptive computer-based accountability test offers a peek at a brave new future

Robert Rothman

A t a time when teachers everywhere are complaining that testing takes too much time away from instruction, the state of Oregon has implemented a test that students can take up to three times a year. And that's just fine with Oregon educators.

That's because the test is administered on computer. Teachers and students receive almost instantaneous results, and the information can be used diagnostically to target students who need further help to meet state standards and provide them with additional instruction. In that way, the state test, which is intended to provide summative information about what students know, also provides some formative information along the way.

"We know you don't fatten a pig by weighing it," says Ted Feller, assistant director of curriculum and student learning for the Centennial School District, a 6,700-pupil district just east of Portland. "But is finding out where a student is taking away a little time [from] instruction? That's the trade-off we make."

Although several states and testing programs have used computer-based assessments, Oregon's testing program, known as Oregon Assessment of Knowledge and Skills (OAKS), is the first statewide testing program that is almost completely online; in 2008–2009, 99.6 percent of the tests were administered on computers. And in January 2009, the U.S. Department of Education approved the use of the online tests for accountability under the No Child Left Behind Act.

The online system offers a number of advantages in addition to rapid results, according to Oregon officials. It provides more accurate information about student performance, particularly for high and low performers. It also reduces the potential for teaching to the test, because test items vary from test to test and from student to student.

At the same time, the use of the test for accountability purposes limits its flexibility, and the current technology restricts the tests to multiple-choice questions, although the state plans to introduce open-ended questions in the future. Although the Oregon system represents a step forward in the use of technology in testing, experts say that step is still a relatively small one when compared with the tremendous potential of newer generations of computer-based assessments.

ADAPTING TO ABILITY

The use of computer-based testing is expanding rapidly in U.S. schools. Half the states have piloted or implemented online end-of-course tests, and the National Assessment of Educational Progress has studied online assessment for future use. Internationally, the Programme for International Student Assessment, a program sponsored by the Organisation for Economic Co-Operation and Development, used an online test to measure reading achievement in 2009. Some assessments under development involve fairly sophisticated systems that use simulations, animation, and other tools that take advantage of technology to engage students in solving complex problems (see "The Next Generation of Assessment").

THE NEXT GENERATION OF ASSESSMENT

What might the next generation of assessments look like? A science assessment offers a clue.

The assessment, known as SimScientists, uses simulations to enable middle-school students to observe natural phenomena, form hypotheses, and create and manipulate environments to test their hypotheses. In that way, educators can assess students' abilities to apply their scientific knowledge in ways not possible on paper-and-pencil tests.

For example, one of the simulations involves an ocean ecosystem. Students are asked to solve problems such as determining the effects of nutrients on algae growth. Students can manipulate the ecosystem in order to test their hypotheses, just as scientists do in the lab. And they must provide evidence to justify their answers.

In this way, teachers get a detailed picture of students' knowledge and their problem-solving abilities, because they can see what students do to solve the problems in real time, says Edys S. Quellmalz, director of technology enhanced assessments and learning systems for WestEd and the project's director.

"You get evidence of problem solving you don't get in a paper-and-pencil environment," Quellmalz says. "'Show your work' isn't quite the same thing."

SimScientists was designed as a formative assessment, one that can help teachers diagnose student needs and adjust instruction accordingly. To that end, it provides students with feedback and offers them opportunities for reflection; for example, it might ask students if the simulation provides them with enough information to answer a particular question. But it can also be used as an interim assessment of what students learned at the end of a curriculum unit.

(continued)

"There is no doubt the methodology exists to develop complex tasks with technical quality that can be part of assessment systems," says Quellmalz. "Clearly, this is the way assessment is moving."

Oregon began to develop a computer-based test in 2001. At the time, the system was offered to districts on a voluntary basis, but districts rapidly signed on because of the prospect of quick results and additional opportunities for students to take the test, according to Tony Alpert, the state's testing director. "That was an incentive to move to online," he says. "We were cutting-edge at that point."

Currently, the computer-based system covers four subjects: English language arts, mathematics, science, and social studies. Under the program, students can take the tests up to three times during the period from October to May, and their highest score counts. Each time a student takes a test, the items are different.

Teachers receive both test scores and achievement-level classifications ("exceeds standard," "meets standard," "nearly meets standard," "does not yet meet standard") for each student. They also receive feedback about how well a student did in particular content strands (such as geometry, algebraic relationships, or measurement). "At the strand level, we are a bit more conservative due to the reduced number of items per strand," notes Steven J. Slater, a specialist in psychometrics in the Oregon Department of Education. "We classify student performance as clearly above standard, clearly below, or not enough information."

Oregon's assessment is an adaptive test, meaning that the questions students answer depend on how they respond; if they answer questions correctly, they are given more difficult questions, and if they cannot, they are given easier questions. Such tests provide more accurate information about student performance than conventional tests, which ask only a limited number of questions at various difficulty levels.

However, the degree of adaptivity is limited. OAKS measures performance relative only to grade-level standards, so there is an upper and a lower limit on the difficulty of the questions that may be posed to students. That limitation was critical for the federal approval of the system for use in accountability, according to Alpert.

Despite this limitation, the adaptive nature of the test offers a number of advantages, according to educators in Oregon. Because each student takes, in effect, a unique test, there is less temptation to focus on particular test items, says Feller. On the old paper-and-pencil test, "if I was a fourth grade teacher, I knew what was on the test, and I could teach that," he says. "This has really stopped us from teaching to the test. It's more content- and skill-based, as opposed to |being based on| test items."

Similarly, the variability in test content discourages cheating, because students do not answer the same questions as those sitting next to them. "Talking to other students is not a good strategy," says Alpert.

ENGAGEMENT AND ECONOMICS

Students appear to like to take tests on computers, according to Alpert. The state department has conducted research that shows that students are answering questions and not simply clicking through the test, he says. "The level of student engagement is higher than on paper," he says.

Moving to an online system has also saved the state money, he notes, although the number of test items and administrations makes it difficult to compare costs with a paper-and-pencil system. "We've added so many features above and beyond what paper-and-pencil tests provide," Alpert says. Administering a paper-and-pencil test three times a year, with instantaneous results, would be "astronomically more." In addition, he adds, "we've saved a few thousand trees."

But districts have borne some of the costs of switching to the system, notes Derek Edens, director of assessment and technology for the David Douglas School District, a 10,000-pupil district southeast of Portland. Districts have had to install fiber-optic lines and update computers to support the system, he says. "Computers have to be no more than three or four years old, or else operating systems are not supported [and] plug-ins are not supported," Edens says. "It takes resources to keep up with the technology."

PATTERNS IN TEST-TAKING

Schools vary in how often and when they administer the online tests. In some cases, says Feller, schools might give the tests to all students in January to gauge their level of achievement. Then, after some instructional interventions, students who did not do well on the first try might retake the test in April. "If teachers decide that [the students] might benefit from a third [administration], they have one in their back pocket," Feller says. "We do not test a kid three times just because we can."

Yet other schools do choose to take advantage of the opportunity for more frequent testing in order to improve their chances for high scores, says Edens. "Some schools feel the necessity, especially with the burden of NCLB, to test all students three times," he says. Because OAKS has been introduced gradually across the state, there are no data that shed light on the effect of online testing on student scores. But educators hope that the formative information provided by the test can give teachers a boost in helping students meet proficiency standards.

Edens and others point out that they have seen little evidence that students who are familiar with computers have an advantage over those with less exposure to them. The level of technological know-how needed to take OAKS is relatively low. In addition, computer knowledge is fairly widespread, even among low-income communities, says Edens. In his district, where 75 percent of students are eligible for free and reduced-price lunch, he says, "I'm not seeing any disadvantage with high-flying kids versus kids in poverty." The district provides professional development for teachers and students to familiarize them with the technology and the test format, and "kids who are new to computers pick it up more easily than adults."

TOWARD NEW TASKS AND PROBLEMS

Edys Quellmalz, director of technology enhanced assessments and learning systems for WestEd, says that computer-based testing can benefit students who are traditionally low performing, as well as students with disabilities and English language learners. Through the use of graphics and sound, advanced computer-based tests can reduce the amount of text in test questions, which often confounds such students, she notes. In addition, complex test items can enable students to respond by drawing or clicking, rather than writing responses. For example, Minnesota's statewide science test uses animation to demonstrate dynamic phenomena such as physics concepts. The test also includes some figural response questions, which may ask students to identify points on a graphic or move objects around.

Such assessments also use technology to engage students in solving complex problems, notes Quellmalz. Although OAKS takes advantage of technology to deliver rapid results and adapt to student responses, it remains limited to multiple-choice questions; it is, in effect, a paper-and-pencil test online. "I worry that the kind of learning that [multiple-choice assessments like OAKS] can test is very constrained: one right answer and highly structured problems," says Quellmalz. "That's [only] a subset of the kinds of tasks and problems we want kids to solve." Newer generations of computer-based assessments, however, offer the possibility of expanding the kind of learning that can be measured online, she notes. By using simulations and web-based resources, testing programs can tap a broad range of higher-order abilities that are difficult to measure with conventional tests. "You can get evidence of problem solving that you couldn't do in a pencil-and-paper environment," she says. "These [tests] provide important ways to broaden what standards are tested and how they are tested."

This chapter originally appeared in the March/April 2010 issue of the Harvard Education Letter.

FOR FURTHER INFORMATION

OAKS Online: www.oaks.k12.or.us

E. S. Quellmalz and J. W. Pellegrino. "Technology and Testing." *Science* 323, no. 5910 (2009): 75–79.

E. S. Quellmalz, M. J. Timms, and B. C. Buckley. *Using Science Simulations to Support Powerful Formative Assessments of Complex Science Learning.* San Francisco: WestEd, 2009.

SimScientists: simscientist.org

B. Tucker. *Beyond the Bubble: Technology and the Future of Student Assessment.* Washington, DC: Education Sector, 2009.

CHAPTER 7

Video Games Take Testing to the Next Level

Researchers see promise in game-like assessments that measure complex skills

Robert Rothman

Young people playing *Halo* or *World of Warcraft* might not realize it, but they are working on the prototypes for a future generation of student tests.

"A video game is nothing but a series of tests," says James Paul Gee, the Mary Lou Fulton Professor of Literacy Studies at Arizona State University and the author of *What Video Games Have to Teach Us About Learning and Literacy*. Game players, he notes, are continually using their knowledge to solve problems. They need to know, for example, how much energy they need to jump over chasms, which tool to use to open doors, and which weapons to use against particular foes. And, Gee says, "At the end, there's a 'super-test'; if you pass, you can take it to a new level."

Based on these principles, Gee and others are currently developing new models of assessment that immerse students in virtual worlds to measure abilities that are difficult, if not impossible, to capture on pencil-and-paper tests, such as the ability to solve problems and conduct scientific inquiry. In some cases, these assessments are also learning experiences, because students receive instantaneous feedback, as players do in actual video games.

In addition, developers say, the assessments document the choices students make with each click of the game device, giving teachers and administrators a wealth of data on student abilities. And unlike performance assessments, which are also designed to capture complex skills like problem solving, they are more practical and less expensive to administer (see "Virtual Versus Performance Assessments").

In many cases, these new assessments are being designed to complement existing state tests for accountability. However, game-based assessments can also be used formatively to help classroom teachers monitor student progress and adjust their instruction according to student needs.

Developers find these game-based assessments appealing because they can provide information on student competencies in problem solving and effective communication—skills that the developers believe are becoming increasingly important. Conventional tests, they note, might tell what a student already knows but tell little about what he or she can do with that knowledge.

Yet it is precisely this advantage that makes the new assessments a difficult sell. Even though the U.S. Department of Education is providing hundreds of millions of dollars to develop new computer-based assessments—which may or may not incorporate gaming aspects—many parents continue to equate learning with what's measured on standardized tests, says Daniel Schwartz, a professor of education at Stanford University. In order to build acceptance of the game-based assessments, researchers and policymakers must make the case for assessing a broader set of student abilities.

VIRTUAL VERSUS
PERFORMANCE ASSESSMENTS

Developers of game-based assessments say that one of their goals is to measure abilities like problem solving that are difficult, if not impossible, to measure with pencil-and-paper tests. But pencil-and-paper performance assessments, like those that ask students to write research papers or conduct science experiments, are intended to measure those abilities as well. Why do some people think the game-based approaches are better?

According to Chris Dede, the Timothy E. Wirth Professor in Learning Technologies at the Harvard Graduate School of Education, and Jody Clarke-Midura, project director for the Virtual Assessment Project at Harvard, game-based assessments offer a number of advantages:

- They are more feasible and less expensive than conventional performance assessments because they are delivered and scored by computer.
- They are standardized, in the sense that they are administered in the same way to every student, unlike paper-and-pencil performance tasks, which require training to ensure that all teachers administer them the same way.
- They enable students to perform tasks that cannot be done in a classroom setting, like manipulating virtual environments to see if the effects matched their hypotheses.
- They provide more complete and accurate information on student abilities because every decision a student makes is recorded. That information is more accurate than asking a student to "show your work." The volume of information also makes the data on student abilities more reliable than the more limited information available from written products.

"We need to come up with new models so that people have a better discourse," says Schwartz. "Learning doesn't mean multiple choice."

MEASURING COMPLEX ABILITIES

The increasing popularity of video and computer games may cause concern among parents, who fear that their children are spending too much time on them. However, educators and researchers increasingly have recognized these games' potential as motivating and engaging learning tools. In a 2005 *Harvard Education Letter* article, Gee noted that games "teach children not only how to play but how to learn, and to keep on learning" (see "The Classroom of Popular Culture").

With that idea in mind, researchers have been designing learning environments using video games. Much of this work has been supported by the John D. and Catherine T. MacArthur Foundation, which since 2006 has awarded $61.5 million to organizations and individuals as part of its Digital Media and Learning program. Perhaps the most ambitious effort is Quest to Learn, a school in New York City in which the curriculum and instructional program are based on game-design principles.

But the developments in assessment are potentially groundbreaking as well. Game-based assessments make it possible to measure complex abilities because they can allow assessors to observe students' activities in ways that are not possible with even the most sophisticated paper-and-pencil tests, says Chris Dede, the Timothy E. Wirth Professor in Learning Technologies at the Harvard University Graduate School of Education.

"Virtual worlds create a rich prompt to students," he says. "They present complicated situations, and students are asked to do things to respond to those complicated situations. And on the back end, you get rich information about student responses."

For example, in one assessment Dede and his colleagues have developed, middle school science students investigate the depletion of a kelp forest in the fictional Kamagua Bay in Alaska. Through the use of an avatar, students take on the persona of a scientist; they walk around the environment and make observations, interact with other characters, and use tools like readings for water temperature and salinity to take measurements. They can choose to change the environment—for example, shut down a power plant—and measure the effects of these changes on kelp growth. And students not only record their decisions, they also indicate why they chose to do what they did.

With these observations, the assessment is able to measure how well the students formed hypotheses, the quality of their observations, and the validity of the inferences they made from these observations—and provide scores on all of these skills, Dede notes. All of these skills are scientific inquiry abilities that organizations such as the National Research Council have said are critical, yet they are difficult or impossible to capture on conventional student tests, he says, and thus game-based assessments can complement existing tests, which measure student knowledge and basic skills effectively.

Arizona State's Gee agrees that the information such assessments provide offers a more nuanced and complete picture of student abilities than conventional tests do. "It's difficult to know what to do with a single score that tells what a student did on Tuesday at 4:00 [when the student took a test]," he says. "Games give scores on a number of variables. They're not scoring whether a student succeeded or failed. They show how the student performed, and in some cases how innovative a solution is."

LEARNING, ASSESSMENT, OR BOTH?

Daniel Schwartz also believes that game-based assessments can measure learning itself. Just as games provide feedback to players to show them how they can get out of a situation in which they find themselves stuck, an assessment can enable students to learn while taking it and measure whether they actually do learn.

To illustrate this idea, Schwartz describes a game-based assessment he and colleagues have developed that asks students to move from booth to booth in a carnival. At the "boss booths," the bosses pose problems to students, such as asking them to design a sealed tank in which both plants and animals can survive, that students must solve in order to move to the next booth. If the students fail to solve the problem correctly, the assessment will indicate why the solution was ineffective; the students can then use resources provided by the game/assessment or even other characters in the game to learn about a better solution. In that way, according to Schwartz, the assessment can measure whether they were effective in seeking additional information.

"A more dynamic image of a learner is an important thing," he says. "What we think learning is, is driven by standardized tests: learning is a state. These things are moving. It's better to measure the slope than the position."

Gee agrees that assessments that are learning experiences are also valuable teaching tools: "An assessment is not useful to a learner if it's not teaching him something."

But Dede, who has helped design game-based assessments intended to measure state and national standards, disagrees with the idea of developing assessments that mix helping students learn with measuring what they know. Dede maintains that fostering students' learning as part of an assessment confounds the measurement of what they already know and can do. He believes learning experiences that provide students feedback as their skills and knowledge grow are important and useful, but that formal diagnostic and summative assessments should focus on measurement, so that they are accurate.

MEETING CHALLENGES

One challenge in designing game-based assessments is coming up with situations that are engaging but not too familiar to students. While they want to create situations that are realistic and perhaps fun so that students will want to engage with them, developers must ensure that some students do not have an advantage because they know more than others about the situation. "Every student knows a little about the ocean and plants, but few students know about kelp forests," Dede says. "It's important to pick a subject matter that provides a level playing field."

Another challenge is managing the voluminous data that the assessments yield. Students make many decisions during the course of these assessments, and each decision is registered on the computer, Schwartz notes. "The density of information is a big deal," he says. To help deal with that problem, Schwartz is exploring whether it is possible to determine students' problem-solving abilities from a few key decision points: "What patterns sort out the kids who did well from the kids who didn't?"

Another challenge is ensuring that the assessments are technically sound and that they provide accurate measures of what they are intended to measure. "A challenge is building a virtual environment so every action has a clearly defined purpose and every student's action can be interpreted as exhibiting knowledge, skills, and attitudes," says Dede. "Which task [indicates] the ability to hypothesize, or make inferences?"

This challenge is particularly acute because of psychometric concerns over reliability—a measure of whether students would get a similar score if they took the same test at a different time. These concerns have tended to favor more traditional measures like multiple-choice tests, which are more likely to be administered in exactly the same way to every student, rather than a complex performance that might yield a different response from different students, depending on the decisions they made along the way. As a result, measures that truly get at complex abilities have been hard to build, suggests Schwartz, adding that the emphasis on reliability "may cut down on our freedom to innovate."

Despite these challenges, the researchers say game-based assessments are feasible and predict that they will become more prevalent in schools in the next few years. Parents of students who do well on conventional tests are looking for more information on how their children are learning, says Schwartz. "I hear from people in Silicon Valley: 'Do you have tests that measure other things we care about, like are students prepared to learn? Do they have deep understanding?' There is a market for this kind of assessment."

"This is undoubtedly where we'll go in the future," predicts Gee.

This chapter originally appeared in the November/December 2010 issue of the Harvard Education Letter.

FOR FURTHER INFORMATION

Researchers at the Virtual Assessment Project in Cambridge, Mass., are developing three virtual assessments with seven school district partners. Watch a video about the development of the Kamagua Bay gamebased assessment on their Web site. www.virtualassessment.org

CHAPTER 8

The Promise of New State Tests

Two consortia plan better tests, but will they lead to better instruction?

Robert Rothman

Beginning in 2014, students in nearly every state will take assessments on computers that will measure their ability to answer complex problems in reading and mathematics. The results will indicate whether they are on track for college and career readiness, and will be compared across state lines. And teachers will have access to a wide range of tools to help them prepare students to meet challenging standards.

That is the vision of two consortia of states that last summer won a total of $330 million from the U.S. Department of Education to begin developing new assessment systems to replace existing state tests. At this point, 44 states (and the District of Columbia) have signed on to one or both of the consortia; they must make a final decision to choose one or neither by the time the assessments are pilot-tested in the 2013–14 school year.

However, in order to realize their promise, the two consortia must work through some difficult technical and educational issues. For instance, they must determine how to design a sequence of assessment components to be administered throughout the course of the year as well as how to implement automated scoring of assessments, says Scott Marion, the associate director of the National Center for the Improvement of Educational Assessment.

"There is the promise of things to be different; they are not different yet," he says. "If people don't think [the new features] are ready for prime time in four years, that will limit what states will be willing to do. States will revert back to what they know. The assessment system will look like a typical assessment system, except administered by computer."

Nevertheless, he and others remain at least cautiously optimistic that the problems can be worked out and that the new assessments will encourage educators to teach higher levels of knowledge and skills. "This is a moment of great opportunity for the country and for children," says Joan L. Herman, the director of the National Center for Research on Evaluation, Standards, and Student Testing at the University of California, Los Angeles.

The grants for the assessment systems were part of the federal Race to the Top program. The Department of Education launched the competition in April, calling for consortia of states to develop assessments that would measure the Common Core State Standards in English language arts and mathematics, which some 40 states and the District Columbia have adopted. Two consortia submitted bids, and both won awards. The Smarter, Balanced Assessment Consortium, (SBAC) led by Washington State, consists of 30 states; the Partnership for the Assessment of Readiness for College and Careers (PARCC), led by Florida, consists of 26 states. (The total adds up to more than 50 because at this point states can join either consortia without committing to administer either test. Several states, including Alaska, Texas, and Virginia are part of neither.)

Although there are some differences between the two consortia's plans, they share many features in common that represent significant departures from current practice. For example, both groups plan to administer assessments primarily on computers, and both would make extensive use of open-ended items, rather than rely almost exclusively on multiple-choice questions, as many current tests do. In addition, both groups plan to develop materials for teachers, such as curriculum maps, to show how the material on the assessments can be taught over the course of the year, and items that can be used formatively in classrooms.

One of the most innovative ideas found in both plans is the proposal to include some tasks in the assessments that would be administered during the school year, in addition to an end-of-course assessment. The PARCC proposal calls for three interim tasks, given at three-month intervals, that are intended to measure topics closer to when students actually study them and provide feedback to students and teachers during the year. The SBAC plan calls for a single extended project to be administered near the end of the year with optional interim assessments.

By administering tasks during the year, the consortia could engage students in higher-level problem solving, such as writing extended research papers or conducting detailed science experiments, says Herman. "This gets us beyond thinking of assessment as a single annual test," she says.

But developing such measures poses substantial challenges, not the least of which is what to include on the interim tasks, notes Marion. The consortia's assessment developers, who include representatives of the participating states, must decide whether these mid-year tasks will measure some of the standards now included on end-of-year tests or whether they will measure mid-term mastery of the standards that will be assessed again at the end of the year, he says.

"If a particular standard [in mathematics, for example] is assessed by a performance task in October, do you go back and assess it in February or May?" Marion asks. "Or do you say, 'I've assessed that standard, and now I'll focus on other standards.' That implies that you don't think kids will develop their performance on that standard from October to May. That seems silly. Why are kids in school?"

Another dramatic change from current practice is the fact that the assessments will be common across states. Each of the states within both the PARCC and the SBAC consortia will administer the same assessments and have agreed to work toward producing results that can be compared across consortia.

That means that the expectations for student performance will be common across states, something that is not the case today, says Herman. "You can move from one state to the next and have consistent standards," she says. "That levels the playing field."

The results can also drive improvements by showing how schools and districts perform relative to other schools and districts using a common metric, suggests Edward Roeber, a professor of education at Michigan State University and a former state testing director. "Normative data can be useful," he says. "Now, high-performing districts can sit on their laurels. [But] If you compare them to other high-performing districts in other states, they may not look so good."

However, Roeber cautions that the potential power of the new assessments could be squandered unless teachers have the knowledge and skills to use assessment data effectively and teach in ways that will lead to higher performance. Although the consortia plan to develop instructional tools, teachers will also need considerable professional development to learn how to teach higher-level skills and knowledge— something few teachers currently teach, he says.

Without this kind of support, he says, "We'll come up with all sorts of comparative data, none of which will help kids learn. We'll have a niftier, more expensive state testing program."

This chapter originally appeared in the November/December 2010 issue of the Harvard Education Letter.

PART III

Technology and School Improvement

CHAPTER 9

"Equity, Access, and Opportunity"

Despite challenges, more districts adopt one-to-one laptop programs

Colleen Gillard

Over the last few years, school districts across the country have initiated one-to-one laptop programs. According to a newly released nationwide survey, more than one-fourth of the 2,500 largest U.S. school districts have at least one full grade of students with their own laptops—a figure that is expected to rise to 50 percent within three years. While the largest one-to-one laptop programs are the districtwide program for grades 6–12 in Henrico County, Va., and Maine's statewide program in middle schools and some high schools, states including Texas, Illinois, Indiana, Massachusetts, Michigan, New Hampshire, New Mexico, Pennsylvania, Vermont, and Florida are also investing in one-to-one computing.

The practical issues involved in implementing these programs are significant, experts say, and so is the expense. In some high-profile cases, districts have canceled programs for either one or the other reason. Nonetheless, many educators believe it's just a matter of time before laptops are as ubiquitous as lunchboxes in students' backpacks.

"It's all about equity, access, and opportunity," says Claudia Mansfield Sutton, a spokeswoman for the American Association of School Administrators, which co-sponsored the nationwide survey, titled *America's Digital Schools 2008* (ADS08). "If a child can only use the computer lab once or twice a week, how can he or she compete? With a laptop, kids can access [digital] content anytime, anywhere."

MIXED RESULTS ON ACHIEVEMENT

Researchers who study one-to-one computing generally like what they see—even if it's hard to measure. There is some preliminary evidence that one-to-one programs lead to improved achievement. Nearly 80 percent of the ADS08 respondents with one-to-one laptop programs reported "moderate to significant" academic gains. Laptop programs have been linked to higher attendance, better discipline, and more effective classroom practices like small-group and project-based learning, in addition to garnering favorable reviews from students, teachers, and parents alike.

Links to higher scores on standardized tests, however, are often difficult to make. "Writing is one of the areas in which the academic benefits are clearest," says Andrew Zucker, a research scientist at the Concord Consortium and author of *Transforming Schools with Technology: How Smart Use of Digital Tools Helps Achieve Six Key Education Goals*. He points to a 2005 study that compared 8th grade writing scores on the Maine Education Assessment before and after the introduction of that state's pioneering laptop program. The study found that laptop users' scores were 75 percent higher.

A 2007 evaluation of 21 middle schools in Texas in the second year of a one-to-one laptop program revealed that while students had fewer disciplinary problems and benefited from more small-group learning than in the 21 middle schools without the laptop program, there were "no significant effects" on their state reading, mathematics, and writing achievement test scores.

"The jury is still out on whether or not [one-to-one programs] add value in student achievement the way it is traditionally measured," says Cheryl Lemke, CEO of the Metiri Group, a consulting firm based in Culver City, Calif., that helps districts pilot and evaluate one-to-one laptop programs. Given how new most programs are, "it's too soon to judge them based on standardized testing," she adds.

MOTIVATION AND ENGAGEMENT

"Students may do well on tests, but we feel these scores are not commensurate with [everything] we think they are learning," concurs Tony Anderson, technology director for the Fullerton School District in Orange County, Calif.

Fullerton is home to the Robert C. Fisler School, a new K–8 school designed around wireless technology and laptop use. At the 900-student school, all students from second to eighth grade have their own laptops. Students in the earlier grades share "COWs" (computers on wheels) or laptop carts carrying about 25 units. Instructional use of technology in the classroom varies from grade to grade.

One recent morning, for example, a seventh grade class was dissecting chicken wings in a lab filled with electronic sensors and probes. Using ProScopes (handheld high-resolution, photo-ready digital microscopes), the students were taking pictures for digital integration into their lab reports. In a second-grade class, children were downloading lessons, answering questions, and then working in groups to finish multimedia presentations before sending them to their teacher's online inbox.

Fisler principal Jackie Pearce believes that laptops promote "self-directed, project-based, and collaborative learning." With students able to work on different things at different rates at different times in a variety of media, she adds, teachers are now better able to meet the diverse needs of the children in their classes and can multitask efficiently between students. "The classroom has never been more exciting," she says.

Education professor David Silvernail, who directs the Center for Educational Policy, Applied Research and Evaluation at the University of Southern Maine, has been studying Maine's middle-school one-to-one laptop program over a seven-year period. Anecdotal evidence from Silvernail's interviews with teachers and students supports Pearce's view. "Student motivation is up, excitement and pride are palpable, and knowledge retention improves when students work on real-world problems," he says. "It's frustrating that we as researchers have trouble quantifying this."

THE CHALLENGES OF GOING DIGITAL

Despite such testimonials, there have also been disappointments and canceled programs in districts across the nation. The Chesterfield County school board in Virginia voted to close its five-year laptop program at the district's pilot high-tech Matoaca High School after determining student test scores hadn't risen sufficiently to justify the roughly $1,500-per-student cost. "We had a mixed response," says Linda Gillespie, director of technology for Chesterfield County Schools. "Some teachers, parents, and students loved it; others didn't." And the Liverpool Central School District outside Syracuse, New York, eliminated its laptop program last year after teachers complained that the devices were little better than distractions, and sometimes worse—as in the cases of students caught exchanging answers on exams or visiting porn sites.

Bette Manchester, director of Maine's $35 million laptop program for middle school students, says she has seen schools in her state flounder as they try to implement the program, due to poor execution, tepid leadership, or inadequate teacher training. "People don't realize it's more about teaching and learning than technology," she says. "They get into trouble when they don't have concrete strategies for implementation [or] clear and specific goals about what they want the technology to do."

Mark Edwards, the new superintendent of North Carolina's Mooresville Graded School District, agrees that leadership and teacher training are critical. As former superintendent of Virginia's Henrico County School District, Edwards is now launching his second district one-to-one laptop program in seven years. He offers several pointers for administrators considering adopting such programs:

- Expect to encounter initial resistance. In particular, taxpayers and others may raise the issue of cost (see "Financing Laptop Programs").
- Begin by visiting other successful one-to-one laptop programs before developing a program appropriate to the needs of your own district.
- Convene an implementation team very early in the process to plan and execute a smooth transition to the new program. Teams should include administrators, principals, and representatives from finance, public relations, human resources, technical support, curriculum, and the facilities departments.
- After programs are up and running, continue to meet semiannually with tech and curriculum directors to review whatever needs adjusting.
- Begin professional development early and differentiate it according to staff members' technological expertise. The main issues, he notes, are likely to have less to do with technology and more to do with curriculum and teaching. Professional development organized around subject areas can help teachers see the relevance of laptops to learning (see "Teaching with One-to-One Laptops").
- Budget collaborative preparation time with in-house technical and curriculum support staff.

FINANCING LAPTOP PROGRAMS

Laptop programs are financed across the country in a variety of creative ways. The states of Maine and Michigan each spent close to $40 million on middle school computing that, like the one-to-one laptop program in Henrico County School District in Virginia, included wiring student homes. Other districts have cobbled together funds from Title 1 federal allocations or state money, along with local business or community grants. Districts in the state of California, whose per-pupil educational budget is among the nation's lowest, ask families to pay $300–$500 a year, with Title 1 scholarship funds available upon request.

In financing the devices in Henrico County, then superintendent Mark Edwards opted for a four-year leasing package that ran nearly $1,400 for an Apple laptop, software, warranty, maintenance, infrastructure/servers, and staff professional development. When amortized over the term of the lease, it amounted to about $350 a year, says Edwards—which he translates to $1 a day. At the end of the four-year contract, families can buy their child's laptop for $40.

Too often districts skimp on professional development, putting programs in jeopardy, says Jeanne Hayes, coauthor of ADS08 and a former teacher who has been tracking technology use in schools for 25 years. "Until teachers buy into it, nothing else matters," she says. While the federal government recommends districts allocate 25 percent of their technology budget for professional development, she notes, typically only 10–12 percent gets spent. Evaluation is also critical to maintaining community support for expensive laptop programs, she says. Although this has been a weak link in the past, she

TEACHING WITH ONE-TO-ONE LAPTOPS

What are teachers' experiences working with one-to-one laptops in the classroom? In his recent book, *Transforming Schools with Technology: How Smart Use of Digital Tools Helps Achieve Six Key Education Goals* (Harvard Education Press, 2008), Andrew A. Zucker notes that "teachers are generally supportive of laptop programs in places where they have been implemented." He cites a 2003 survey of 3,000 teachers in Maine, in which 70 percent of the respondents agreed that laptops helped them meet curricular goals more effectively and individualize curricula to better meet students' needs.

Among the benefits to teachers, Zucker lists:

- *Stimulating student engagement.* A Michigan teacher of high-risk students observes, "I saw more excitement and willingness to work, and the quality of the work was greatly improved."
- *Offering more flexibility in the classroom.* For instance, a teacher can pull out a spreadsheet for a few minutes in the middle of a lesson without having to reserve a computer lab ahead of time.
- *Providing instantaneous feedback to students.* "This feedback helps the teachers identify and work with students who need extra attention," Zucker writes.
- *Granting access to more up-to-date information.* A teacher in Maine says, "It's like having an interactive textbook that never becomes obsolete."
- *Enhancing professional productivity.* Teachers use computers to more efficiently design and create materials, prepare lesson plans, diagnose student weaknesses, and communicate with colleagues, parents, and students.

continued

Zucker also points out challenges for teachers in making the transition to one-to-one computing:

- *Adjusting instructional practices.* Typically this involves "greater sharing and collaboration among teachers," he notes.
- *Developing new lessons that use laptops.* This includes learning to use the computers, the Internet, and software effectively and being able to advise students about computer use. If a student forgets his or her laptop, teachers also need to have a backup lesson plan ready.
- *Rethinking classroom management.* One-to-one computing can introduce new disruptions; for instance, laptop batteries may need to be recharged at school. And even with Internet filtering software, Zucker notes, students can browse sites not germane to the lesson. "Being the iBook police is hard," one Henrico County teacher says.

Adapted from *Transforming Schools with Technology: How Smart Use of Digital Tools Helps Achieve Six Key Education Goals*, by Andrew A. Zucker (Harvard Education Press, 2008).

says this year's survey shows schools are paying more attention to evaluation.

PROTOCOLS FOR PROPER USE

Parents and teachers may raise other common concerns—for instance, that students will lose the devices or use them inappropriately. Clearly defined protocols can make a big difference. Fisler School principal Pearce begins each school year with parent-child assemblies on laptop protocols, in which she goes over school rules about the care and handling of laptops, internet safety, and web etiquette. Such protocols require that computers arrive in school with batteries charged and in their protective sleeves and ask that laptops never be placed on the ground or used in the cafeteria.

Many educators agree that full-time in-house computer support is essential to manage minor repairs and handle software glitches. Maine researcher Silvernail found that schools with clearly defined equipment-use protocols reported losing only 1 to 2 percent of their laptops to theft, loss, or breakage.

Schools may also need to invest in software or technology to detect inappropriate computer use. At the Fisler School, internal servers monitor web use and email the principal's office anytime a student is found to have slipped past the server's filters to visit inappropriate sites or download games.

Despite the expense and challenges of one-to-one computing, educators and researchers increasingly believe that—done right—the benefits can outweigh the drawbacks. "If it's about leveling the playing field or increasing student achievement, we feel it's been very effective," Silvernail says.

This chapter originally appeared in the May/June 2008 issue of the Harvard Education Letter.

FOR FURTHER INFORMATION

America's Digital Schools 2008: The Six Trends to Watch. Available online at www.ads2008.org

Fullerton School District Laptop Program. www.fsd.k12.ca.us/menus/1to1/index.ssi

D. Silvernail and A.K. Gritter. "Maine's Middleschool Laptop Program: Creating Better Writers—Research Brief." The Center for Education Policy, Applied Research, and Evaluation (CEPARE), University of

Southern Maine, Gorham, ME, October 2007. Available online at
www.usm.maine.edu/cepare/

M. Warschauer. *Laptops and Literacy: Learning in the Wireless Classroom*. New York: Teachers College Press, 2006.

A. Zucker. *Transforming Schools with Technology: How Smart Use of Digital Tools Helps Achieve Six Key Education Goals*. Cambridge, MA: Harvard Education Press, 2008.

CHAPTER 10

Learning Across Distance

Virtual-instruction programs are growing rapidly, but the impact on "brick-and-mortar" classrooms is still up in the air

Kristina Cowan

Online education is undergoing a sea change in the state of Florida. Starting in 2009–2010, any student who meets certain eligibility requirements will be able to attend school virtually, thanks to legislation enacted last July. Florida's 67 school districts will be required to offer full-time virtual instruction for K–8 students and full-time or supplemental instruction for grades 9–12. Districts may develop virtual-education programs themselves or in collaboration with other districts, or they may contract with accredited providers approved by the Florida Department of Education. The mandate is intended to extend a state program that started as a pilot in 2003–2004 to the district level. The pilot program offered only two providers, Florida Virtual Academy and Florida Connections Academy, and capped the number of K–8 students who could enroll in online courses.

Florida's new mandate for districts is only the latest development in a trend that began a decade ago. At that time, according to Susan Patrick, president and CEO of the Vienna,

Va.-based North American Council for Online Learning (NA-COL), the biggest driver behind online programs was demand for specialized or advanced courses that were otherwise unavailable in local schools. A 2008 report, "Keeping Pace with K–12 Online Learning," commissioned by NACOL and others, defines online learning as "teacher-led education that takes place over the Internet, with the teacher and student separated geographically." The term "distance learning" includes online education (Florida's legislation calls it "virtual" education), but is considered a broader category that includes use of computers, television, or satellites to deliver instruction.

Online education can be synchronous, with teachers and students communicating in real time, or asynchronous, with students working at different times. Some online programs are supplemental, used by students otherwise enrolled in regular classes, while others are full-time, for students working at home. According to the 2008 "Keeping Pace" report, 44 states offer significant full-time or supplemental online-learning options for students, and six states don't offer either.

ONE MILLION AND COUNTING

Though the exact number of students enrolled in online courses is unknown, knowledgeable estimates put the figure at 1 million, according to NACOL. Student populations run the gamut, educators say, from advanced students wanting to accelerate to students struggling academically or socially, and may include young mothers, students with restrictive medical conditions, or those in arts or sports who need flexible schedules. Two of the biggest providers are the Florida Virtual School (FLVS) and Herndon, Va.-based K12 Inc. Founded in 1997 as the country's first statewide online public high school, FLVS delivered 137,000 half-credit courses to approximately 63,600 students during the 2007–2008 academic year; K12 served more than 40,000 full-time K–12 students in 17 states and the District of Columbia. Most state-sponsored programs offer supplemental courses, and course enrollments ranged from a few thousand to about 10,000 in 2007–2008, depending on the state, according to the NACOL-sponsored report.

Florida is the third state to issue a mandate regarding online learning. In 2006, the Michigan legislature passed a requirement that students spend at least 20 hours learning online before graduation, either by taking an online course or by doing online course assignments in their regular classes. Beginning with the class of 2009–2010, students in Alabama will have to take and pass one "online-enhanced" core or elective course to graduate, which means a course using Internet technology on a regular basis. These online-enhanced courses may be delivered in several ways: through a "teacher-led" experience, with students in a lab at one school receiving video instruction from a teacher located at another school—also known as "interactive videoconferencing"—or through "blended" instruction, where students and teachers are located in the same classroom, with students completing some work online. Students in a blended course might, for example, work outside the classroom in virtual teams with students from other schools or classrooms to learn writing, research, teamwork, and technology skills.

Supporters of these new mandates say the impetus is to help students develop the technological skills they will need in college and to offer courses that might otherwise be unavailable locally. In Florida, expanding choice for parents and students was also a top priority. "This is the wave of the future," says Connie Milito, chief government relations officer for the Hillsborough County Public Schools in Tampa, Fla. "This is just another way to offer choice to families."

BENEFITS AND DRAWBACKS

As online programs expand, some of the benefits and trade-offs of online education are becoming clear.

Supporters of online education point to flexible scheduling and the ability to tailor courses for each student as the top benefits. Patrick, president of NACOL, says that offering online learning also expands the number of courses available to students and increases their access to highly qualified teachers.

Oakman High School in rural Walker County, Ala., for example, has expanded its foreign-language offerings through online education, according to principal Joel Hagood. In the past, Oakman offered only French, but now the school uses AC-CESS (Alabama Connecting Classrooms, Educators and Students Statewide), a state-sponsored distance-learning initiative launched in fall 2005, to offer Spanish courses—something many parents wanted. Through ACCESS, an Alabama-certified teacher at one school provides instruction to students in another school via interactive videoconferencing and the Internet.

The flexibility of online learning is also a plus for nontraditional students, says Suzanne Williams, a high school English teacher with the Electronic Classroom of Tomorrow. The online public school based in Columbus, Ohio, serves K–12 students throughout the state. Students are able to create their own schedules, she notes, which is a big help to those with special circumstances, such as teenage parents. Williams says about 20 to 25 of the 160 students she teaches are pregnant or have children.

But others warn of drawbacks. Dennis Van Roekel, president of the National Education Association in Washington, D.C., says when online courses create or extend learning opportunities—such as for a student in rural Alaska taking calculus online—that's a good thing, but they shouldn't replace the classroom experience, as the full-time program in Florida would do. "When you start using online courses as a total alternative, you lose all the benefits of the face-to-face interaction, . . . [the] sense of community, social development, and the variety of instructional methods," Van Roekel explains.

Mark Pudlow, spokesman for public policy advocacy at the Florida Education Association in Tallahassee, Fla., says brick-and-mortar schools expose children to diversity, an important aspect of socialization that's difficult to recreate online. "When you go to public schools, you interact with [different people] and you get to see how [they] look at the same situation. That's very important to the health of our nation," Pudlow says. "I worry that in a virtual situation, even though parents make sure a kid goes to soccer practice or church, it's not the same as a public school situation."

DETERMINING QUALITY AND EFFECTIVENESS

Assessing the quality of online programs is a key concern among educators. Most providers are accredited by one of six recognized regional accrediting agencies, and states and school districts review providers before allowing their credits to transfer to school transcripts, says Patrick. Full-time programs are usually responsible for their students' scores on state assessments required by No Child Left Behind. For those in supplemental courses, the brick-and-mortar school where they're enrolled is responsible for the tests. Still, NACOL's research indicates that many states lack sophisticated data on the long-term performance of students taking online courses. According to NACOL's 2007 "National Primer on K–12 Online Learning," "A mechanism to track online programs and students is an apparent first-level policy requirement that a surprising number of states have not yet put into place."

Researchers disagree on whether there is a sufficient body of research on the effectiveness of virtual learning. A 2005 report by the North Central Regional Educational Laboratory says the available research seems to show that academically, online students perform as well as or better than traditional students. But given the small number of studies, the report notes, "we cannot have real 'confidence' in these conclusions until there is much more support available from high-quality quantitative research."

Dr. Wayne Blanton, executive director of the Florida School Boards Association in Tallahassee, Fla., believes much more research needs to be conducted before drawing conclusions about the effectiveness of online education. "Virtual learning is very young. It's in its infant stage compared to the age of the educational system itself," Blanton says. But Dr. Bror Saxberg, chief learning officer at K12, offers a different take. "To a large extent, that argument should now be over," he says. He believes that ample research shows online learning and traditional education are equally effective, as long as online programs are set up properly, with strong teachers.

In July 2008, the U.S. Department of Education released a guide to help schools evaluate K–12 online-education programs. Because of the rapid expansion of programs and the "dearth of existing research on the topic, it is critical to conduct rigorous evaluations of online learning in K–12 settings to ensure that it does what people hope it will do: help improve student learning," the report says.

WHO BENEFITS?

Ask Tracy Hall, in her sixth year of teaching with the Florida Virtual Academy (FLVA), who benefits most from online learning and she'll point to two groups: advanced students and struggling students. In a traditional classroom—where Hall taught for six years before joining FLVA—most teaching is geared to those who are academically in the middle, she says, in the hope that advanced and slower students will still learn something. But in an online environment, advanced students can experience higher levels of responsibility and bigger challenges, and they perform very well, Hall notes. Struggling students also benefit from one-on-one time with both teachers and parents in an online setting.

Williams, the teacher with the Electronic Classroom of Tomorrow, agrees that one-on-one support is a boon, especially for struggling students. Students embarrassed to ask for help in front of others in a traditional classroom don't confront that situation online, Williams says. "They can just call me"—and they do, sometimes as early as 7 a.m. or as late as 10 p.m.

"Having been in the classroom, I can tell you that one thing—one strategy, one tool—rarely works for all 30 students," says Hall. "So when you have a child [learning] at home, it's really what works for that one student. All the decisions are made based on what's best for the child. The teacher, parent, school [decide together] what they think is best for the child." Students less likely to benefit from virtual classes are those whose parents aren't active in the process, Hall says. Parents have to commit time and effort to help the child succeed.

Experts across the board tend to agree that online learning is not the best option for every student. Some benefit greatly from online education, while others perform best in traditional classrooms. Clayton M. Christensen, professor of business administration at Harvard Business School and coauthor of *Disrupting Class: How Disruptive Innovation Will Change the Way the World Learns*, predicts a blended system will ultimately prevail. "People will still go to school buildings, but much of the learning will be offered online, and the role of the teacher in the physical classroom will change over time from the sage on the stage to the guide on the side—to be a mentor, motivator, and coach," he says. "The teacher will

VIRTUAL LEARNING IN FLORIDA

- School districts shall provide full-time virtual instruction to eligible students in grades K–8 and either full-time or part-time virtual courses in grades 9–12.

- Districts are responsible for providing equipment and Internet connections to full-time students, where appropriate.

- Certified teachers must provide at least 85 percent of a student's instruction.

- Students can participate if they were enrolled in public school during the previous year, or transferred into the state within the past 12 months as military dependents.

- Kindergartners can participate only if they were previously enrolled in publicly funded preK programs for disabled children or children of teenage parents, or if they are repeating kindergarten.

- Attendance is recorded daily or at times determined by the local school board.

- Special education students may participate as part of the continuum of services required of each district. However, "not every individual school, including the School District Virtual Instruction Program, is required to have the resources and capacity to serve all students."

- For reporting purposes, a district virtual instruction program is considered one school.

Source: "School District Virtual Instruction Program (HB7067) Questions and Answers," Florida Department of Education.

work individually with many students, diagnose what learning needs they have, and help them find the best online course or resources to help them and motivate them. It will be a very different system, but it should be a much more rewarding system for everyone.

"Simply moving monolithic instruction online and delivering it in the same way won't do the trick ultimately," he adds. "The real key and causal mechanism is to make it student-centric—able to customize [instruction] for different students with different learning needs, motivations, intelligences, aptitudes, and learning styles."

This chapter originally appeared in the January/February 2009 issue of the Harvard Education Letter.

FOR FURTHER INFORMATION

C.M. Christensen, M.B. Horn and C.W. Johnson. *Disrupting Class: How Disruptive Innovation Will Change the Way the World Learns*. New York: McGraw Hill, 2008.

"Evaluating Online Learning: Challenges and Strategies for Success," U.S. Department of Education Office of Educational Technology, 2008. Available online at: www.ed.gov/admins/lead/academic/evalonline/index.html

North American Council for Online Learning www.nacol.org

J. Watson. "Keeping Pace with K–12 Online Learning: A Review of State-Level Policy and Practice," Learning Point Associates/North Central Regional Educational Laboratory, 2005.

J. Watson, B. Gemin and J. Ryan. "Keeping Pace with K–12 Online Learning: A Review of State-Level Policy and Practice," Evergreen Consulting Associates, 2008. Available online at: www.kpk12.com

CHAPTER 11

Hybrid Schools for the iGeneration

New schools combine "bricks" and "clicks"

Brigid Schulte

School buses begin pulling up in front of Carpe Diem, a middle and high school in Yuma, Ariz., around 7:15 in the morning. In the next 30 minutes, 273 students in crisp uniforms will walk through the front doors and have their ID badges scanned to record their attendance.

By 7:45, most will be sitting in front of computers at their work stations—row upon row of individual study carrels in a big open space administrators call the Learning Center. Middle school students sit on one side of the room, high school students on the other, separated by an area with cushy couches and tables called the Fishbowl, where students gather to chat between classes or to work on group projects.

For the next 55 minutes, students work independently at their computers, learning core subjects or electives through online curricula aligned to Arizona's state standards. They put on headphones or twist iPod ear buds into their ears, because the online programs are interactive and multimodal—comprised of audio, video vignettes, flash animation, quizzes, and games. Paraprofessionals called "assistant coaches" walk through the center to make sure kids are doing their work, fix computer glitches, help with academic questions, and—most importantly, administrators say—check in emotionally with the students, talking with them about anything at home or at school that might be affecting their learning.

The students may be sitting in the same place, but, academically, they're all over the map. The online curriculum for each course is adaptive, meaning it can gauge from the students' answers when they have mastered something and are ready to move ahead and when they may need extra practice before moving on. A bar on the upper right corner of the screen tracks students' progress in every course and becomes part of a report automatically e-mailed to parents at the end of every week.

Using this "daily achievement data" from the students' online work, teachers at Carpe Diem meet with students individually or in small groups, called workshops, to give either extra remedial help or to facilitate enrichment projects. Grouped roughly by age, students rotate in and out of the Learning Center, workshops, gym, or science labs every 55 minutes until the end of the day.

While the workshops tend to be age- or grade-specific, they can also be based on a broad concept and pull students in across all levels, says founder Rick Ogston. "Last year, we had a schoolwide project in which students learned about the Renaissance period through music, poetry, costume, food and [by] building a life-size trebuchet. We then had a Renaissance Fair outside." Every day is different, Ogston says, though on average students spend 50 to 70 percent of their time in front of the computer. "There is a lot of flexibility," he says, "which is hard for people to wrap their traditional minds around."

A NEW KIND OF SCHOOL

Carpe Diem, a public charter school, is an entirely new type of school and one of only a handful of its kind that have sprung up in recent years across the United States. They seek to combine the best of traditional, face-to-face instruction with the best of the cutting-edge online curriculum available to virtual schools. The result is something education experts are calling a hybrid school.

Instead of a traditional brick-and-mortar school, or the completely online clicks of a virtual school (see "Learning Across Distance," *Harvard Education Letter*, January/February 2009), hybrids are also sometimes referred to as bricks-and-clicks schools. Unlike blended learning, where some students in traditional schools may take one or two courses online per semester in addition to their regular classes, hybrid schools typically divide up the learning in such a way that students spend at least half the day learning on a computer and rarely sit in large classrooms where everyone learns the same subject at the same time (see "Incorporating Online Learning: Existing Models").

Ogston says he came up with the idea for the school while he was running a small charter school that was based on character education and building personal relationships between teachers and students. "I was discouraged. We were not as effective as we needed to be," he says. "We didn't tap into the learners and learning styles of all the kids coming to our schools. That's the underpinning of the entire idea for the school now. It's designed for the 'iGeneration.'"

Ogston felt that technology, which was so ubiquitous in his students' lives outside of school, needed to be a part of his vision for this new kind of school. "But it couldn't be a matter of infusing computers and letting them play around a little bit. It had to be disruptive, a complete change." So he put smart boards, projectors, laptops, and online student response systems into classrooms. He sought out the most innovative online curriculum that was adaptive, engaging, rigorous, and aligned with state standards. He brought his charter school

INCORPORATING ONLINE LEARNING: EXISTING MODELS

The online learning world is growing so rapidly that even experts are struggling with how to define the different models that are emerging. Still, many agree that schools generally fall along the following continuum:

Technology-Infused Traditional Schools. In these schools, students learn primarily from teachers in classrooms, but they may also go to computer labs or use programs such as Skype or Blackboard.

Blended Learning in Traditional Schools. Sometimes also referred to as the "online buffet" model, these are traditional schools that allow students to take a few of their courses online.

Hybrid Schools. These schools combine both online curriculum and face-to-face (F2F) teaching. Students go to a physical school but spend much of the day on the computer working at their own pace using online curricula that can be highly individualized. Teachers work with students one on one or in small groups to reinforce skills or extend learning through projects and other types of activities.

Virtual Schools. These schools are completely online. Students typically work at home, supervised by a parent or adult; teachers, who also work at home, may be in another state. Instruction may be synchronous, with students learning directly from a teacher online, or asynchronous, with students working online and e-mailing or talking to teachers by phone at a later time.

teachers in on the project, training them to take on an entirely new kind of teaching role.

Ogston also disrupted the traditional school week. Students on track go to school Monday through Thursday from 7:45 until 4 p.m. Students who are home sick or out of town with family can keep up with their studies online. Students who have fallen behind are required to go to "Friday school."

After five years operating in this disruptively different way, the results are impressive. For two consecutive years, Carpe Diem, which is a majority minority school (more than half of all students also qualify for free or reduced-price lunches), led the state in the amount of growth students showed on test scores. Arizona has designated it a "highly performing" school. Its graduation rate continues to increase, as does the number of students going to college. It has won rave reviews from parents at greatschools.com, kudos from *Business Week*, and a bronze-star ranking from *U.S. News and World Report*.

And just as Carpe Diem is making its impressive gains, other hybrid schools are opening up or in the works. New York recently opened the pilot School of One program that combines teacher time with individualized online learning. Rocketship Education, a pioneer in hybrid schools, opened two K–5 charter schools in 2007 and 2009 for low-income English-language learners in San Jose, Calif. The schools are working so well—they are among the top-performing low-income schools in the state—that Rocketship has won $7 million in grants to open 30 new hybrid charter schools nationwide by 2015.

THE END OF "FACTORY" INSTRUCTION

Central to the hybrid model is advocates' belief that online curricula developed over the past 15 years for virtual schools—like Dream Box and Reasoning Mind—allow students to work at their own pace while freeing teachers from curriculum planning, assessment, classroom management, and having to "teach to the middle" in large, diverse classrooms. Instead, teachers can focus on what they do best: interacting with students.

"We reserve teacher time for all those wonderful things that only teachers can do—guided instruction, group discussion, helping kids learn to listen to each other and challenge each other, helping higher order, critical thinking," says Rocketship's spokeswoman, Judith McGarry. "But at the same time, we think individualized learning requires more than great teaching. It's unfair to put that burden, as we have in our society, on teachers. Every child learns differently. That recognition led us to learn how computers can assist in individualizing learning."

"We have blown up the classroom," says Mark Kushner, founder of the Flex Academy, a hybrid high school that opened in San Francisco last fall. "The era of factory-model instruction is over. No more going to classes all day in large groups whether the students need that class or not. Our kids love it because they're sick of sitting in a class that they either don't understand or don't need. It's like Goldilocks. It was either too fast or too slow. And hybrids like the Flex Academy are just right."

Interest in hybrids took off in 2009 after the U.S. Department of Education released a meta-analysis of online learning studies that appeared to confirm that a blend of face-to-face teacher time with online curriculum produced better outcomes than either face-to-face time alone or online learning alone, according to Susan Patrick, who heads the advocacy group International Association for K–12 Online Learning (iNacol).

The federal study also emboldened reform groups like the Digital Learning Council, headed by former governors Jeb Bush (R-Fla.) and Bob Wise (D-W.Va.), to embrace hybrid schools as a way to reform schools while helping them operate more cost-effectively.

"This is the time of the moment joining with the means," says Wise. "The moment is greater demands for student outcomes and a crisis in education funding, and the means is the ability to rapidly scale-up to use technology effectively to assist the teacher and the public education process."

ONLY FOR THE MOTIVATED?

Critics and skeptics, however, argue that while online programs might work well for motivated, high achievers who want to take advanced courses, they won't necessarily work as well for younger students who are not as intrinsically motivated or lack the time-management skills of older students. They note that the Department of Education meta-analysis concentrated on studies of online learning in colleges and universities simply because there are so few K–12 studies.

"We think technology, online learning, is essential for kids to understand, because it's the world they live in," says Andrea Prejean, associate director for education policy and practice at the National Education Association. "But we're concerned with the notion that this is how we're going to fix schools when we're not exactly sure how it's even going to work. Going slow to go fast is not a bad thing here."

Robert Pianta, an expert in early childhood education and assessing teacher quality and dean of the Curry School of Education at the University of Virginia, says that while he has real concerns about virtual schools, he sees promise in the hybrid model as long as the right balance between online and teacher-led instruction can be found. "And I don't know where the tipping point is," he says. "We have goals for kids being in school that go beyond just their performance on achievement tests. To the degree that schools are also trying to help kids make decisions, become good citizens, foster leadership skills and how to negotiate complex personal interactions, you need engagement with other people and to be around adults who can help scaffold that learning."

Hybrid schools appear to allow for that, he says, while making use of technology in the most efficient way. Allowing third graders to learn multiplication tables with an online program rather than sitting through a whole class lesson is something that Pianta sees as having real merit. But, he says, "we've just got to be really careful about preserving space in the educational experience to learn those kinds of social skills which are ultimately very necessary in a community. We have to be careful about unintended consequences."

"IT'S WHERE WE ARE HEADING"

Because online learning and hybrid schools are so new, there is little research showing their effectiveness. And even advocates worry that the growth is outstripping policy makers' ability to ensure that all programs are high quality, meet national core and state standards, are properly audited, and are held accountable for student outcomes. For instance, some schools, like Carpe Diem and Rocketship, use interactive online learning for the technology part of the hybrid. Others simply videotape teacher lectures and call it online learning, iNacol's Patrick says.

Although licensing online software, which is constantly updated, is costly, some hybrid schools are less expensive than traditional schools—with fewer teachers required and smaller capital costs, Patrick said. Because Rocketship Education, for example, does not need certified teachers to supervise its online Learning Center, it has reduced staffing by five teachers and five classrooms, saving $500,000 a year over traditional schools, according to McGarry.

Richard Ferdig, a professor at Kent State University who studies online learning, says the question to ask is not whether hybrid schools are better than traditional or online schools but which method works best in which circumstances and for which students. In studies of online and traditional learning in Wisconsin, he found that students learning Algebra I online performed significantly better than students in a traditional setting. Yet students learning Algebra II from a classroom teacher performed significantly better than students who learned it online.

Ferdig says the results depended on the quality of the curriculum and the difficulty of conveying certain concepts online. "The Algebra I online curriculum had cool tools, widgets and demos. And Algebra II, which requires complex charts and graphs, was more difficult to convey online. In a chat room, you can't really do complex drawings or charts," he said. "Does that mean Algebra II should only be taught face to face? No. But if you teach it online, then you have to take these issues into consideration."

"We have success stories for face-to-face schools and blended or hybrid schools and for virtual schools," Ferdig says. "It's more about under what conditions is each of these successful? I won't go on record saying hybrid is the best, but I think that's where we are heading. You go back to what makes a classroom successful. You provide kids with relevant content that they can own and connect to the real world, and opportunities to engage with others—whether that is kids in the same classroom or across the world. And now we have innovative means to be able to seek content in new ways. I don't care how engaging a teacher you are, we now have technology that showcases molecules in 3-D, which opens opportunities for kids to explore."

Barbara Means, the SRI researcher who authored the federal meta-analysis, says that only time—and further study—will tell whether hybrid schools really will be the wave of the future. "If we end up having the high-performing KIPP [Knowledge Is Power Program] equivalent for the bricks-and-clicks schools, then I think more districts will be interested in establishing them," she said. "But if some really strong providers don't emerge and there isn't good evidence with respect to effectiveness, hybrids will remain marginal."

AN OPEN QUESTION

At the Flex Academy, students sit at their computer carrels under the grand crystal chandeliers of San Francisco's old Press Building, hang out on cushy couches, or take their laptops to the mahogany bar that serves as their Internet cafe before heading out to classrooms. They can eat organic food at the cafeteria or go to any of the nearby bistros for lunch.

Kushner and other hybrid advocates may have blown up the classroom, but whether what they've replaced it with really works—and will work for large segments of the school-age population—remains an open question. What is clear, however, is that hybrid schools won't feel old school, so to speak. They'll look, in part, like something most adults know only too well.

"Going to a hybrid school is just like going to work," Kushner says. "The kids go to their desks, they turn on their computers, they read things, they read e-mails, they go online, they go to meetings—only these meetings are classes designed for them."

This chapter is adapted from an article that appeared in the March/April 2011 issue of the Harvard Education Letter.

FOR FURTHER INFORMATION

M. B. Horn and H. Staker. *The Rise of K–12 Blended Learning*. Mountain View, CA: Innosight Institute, 2011. Available online at www .innosightinstitute.org

B. Means et al. *Evaluation of Evidence-Based Practices in Online Learning: A Meta-Analysis and Review of Online Learning Studies*. Washington, D.C.: U.S. Department of Education, 2009. Available online at www2.ed.gov/rschstat/eval/tech/evidence-based-practices/finalreport.pdf

CHAPTER 12

Like Teacher, Like Student

**Online PD helps teachers learn to collaborate
so their students will, too**

Dave Saltman

I n Robbinsville, N.J., fourth-grade teacher Linda Biondi helps teachers share and critique each other's essays on the National Writing Project's digital writing websites. Back in the classroom, she works with her students to do the same thing—encouraging each other to dig deeper within themselves for details as they master their writing skills.

Meanwhile, middle school teachers in Arizona work together via a video link, sharing materials, ideas, and feedback as they learn how to teach a new community problem-solving unit on highway safety, uploading their finished unit materials to a state-sponsored portal. As part of the unit, students in these teachers' classrooms engage in similar collaborative activities, uploading their finished work to the district's website.

And in California, a website launched by the state in September 2010 called Brokers of Expertise offers a place for the state's teachers to share their lessons, communicate their ideas about teaching, and seek advice and guidance from other teachers.

These days, everyone is trying to get students to think about their own thinking—and take that thinking to a higher level. To do this, educators are urging teachers to help students teach—and even assess—each other, since the success of so-called student-centered instruction is predicated on getting students to collaborate and take charge of their own learning.

So it is important, experts say, that teachers, too, understand how to learn from their peers. And where better to understand collaboration than in a virtual environment? By necessity, online efforts require teacher-participants to reach out to each other in very deliberate ways, such as through e-mail or postings, if they are to share the workload or solve problems. Whether working together in cyberspace on a research paper, responding to comments online, or searching for information on the Web and then sharing that information with unseen colleagues, the common theme today in online professional development (OPD) is teaching teachers about collaboration.

"STICKY" PD

Online professional development is "not just about learning things from the computer, but from each other, and how that connects to student-centered learning," says Will Richardson, the popular speaker, teacher-blogger, and author of *Blogs, Wikis, Podcasts, and Other Powerful Web Tools*. Richardson also develops and runs OPD workshops. "Physical-space PD wasn't 'sticky' and didn't model the type of learning we expect kids to do," he says. Because the OPD he has developed with a partner is "long-term PD in online social spaces," teachers evolve a willingness to self-direct their own development as a response to learning in that kind of environment, Richardson says.

Other experts working to train teachers online agree. "One of the hallmarks of online learning is that it changes the onus of learning from the teacher to the student," observes Dr.

Lynne Meeks, who runs Alabama's portion of eLearning for Educators, a federally funded multistate ODP project.

Notably, the recently released National Education Technology Plan calls for more online PD offerings. In the federal vision, "episodic and ineffective professional development is replaced by professional learning that is collaborative, coherent, and continuous, and that blends more effective in-person courses and workshops with the expanded opportunities, immediacy, and convenience enabled by online environments full of resources and opportunities for collaboration."

Teachers typically do not interact with each other during the day as much as they do with their students. A multiweek OPD course, for example, can provide the structure for regular, formalized contact between teachers—and a basis for collaboration—that daily teaching itself never provides. Likewise, online communities, such as those offered by the National Writing Project or Brokers of Expertise, offer a place to go to try out ideas with colleagues any time of the day or week.

ELIMINATING THE "INTIMIDATION FACTOR"

Another benefit of online peer-to-peer learning is its partial anonymity. Jacob Hesselschwardt, a middle school teacher who works virtually with teachers around Louisiana to help raise student test scores through an online course, says "the intimidation factor" that might arise when one colleague disagrees with another is softened in a virtual setting, where opinions are written down, and then responded to, and those responses are commented on, adding more nuance and value to the exchange.

Other teachers say that online discussions that include teachers from the same school can even promote collegiality when teachers are offline. Lauren Kenney, a Fremont, N.H., K–8 technology teacher who has both taken courses with and facilitated courses for Open NH, finds that teacher-participants become resources for each other and—if working in the same school—may continue to collaborate outside of the PD venue, strengthening the school as a community.

"Since the professor or facilitator isn't always immediately available, OPD encourages collaboration and connectivity among participants and colleagues," explains Kenny. "I have had several of the teachers in my school come to me for ideas and with requests for collaboration as a result of participating in an online professional development course with them."

To be effective, OPD requires immediate connection to classroom practice, and then a reconnection with peers—something the collaborative qualities inherent in the best OPD support, asserts Richard Elmore, Harvard University's Gregory R. Anrig Professor of Educational Leadership. He points to Ultranet, the official portal for teachers in Victoria, Australia, as a good example of a professional development site that allows teachers to network effectively and supports their interactions with each other, thereby enriching their practice (see "OPD Websites").

OBSTACLES AND QUESTIONS

However, several obstacles remain in spreading the gospel of collaboration through OPD. In particular, many teachers may not have the technological know-how to participate, regardless of their level of motivation.

Recent U.S. Department of Education statistics show teachers found professional development of any kind about educational technology useful, but a majority took relatively few instructional hours. This is supported by a 2010 *Education Week* analysis of school- and district-level data, as reported to the Department of Education: 91 percent of school districts *offer* professional development in using Internet resources and tools for instruction, but just 15 percent *require* this form of PD.

OPD WEBSITES

- The Math Forum @ Drexel: mathforum.org
- National Science Digital Library: nsdl.org
- National Writing Project: www.nwp.org
- Open NH (New Hampshire): www.opennh.net
- IDEAL (Arizona): www.ideal.azed.gov/p
- Brokers of Expertise (California): www.myboe.org
- Ultranet (Australia): www.education.vic.gov.au

Still, recent research on OPD suggests that helping teachers overcome technical obstacles to using it may be worth it. In a series of randomized trials between 2007 and 2009, for example, researchers at Boston College documented a larger increase in teacher knowledge—with smaller, yet significant, effects on some measures of student knowledge—among math and English language arts teachers who participated in 100 hours of OPD, as compared with those in a control group who simply continued with their regular PD. The researchers are currently conducting secondary data analyses to examine the conditions under which OPD is most effective.

Anthropologist Wesley Shumar, who works with Drexel University's Math Forum—a pioneer in OPD—notes that introducing teachers to the online environment before they take Math Forum courses has reduced the often alienating aspect of impersonal virtual space. "We started offering online orientation sessions so that teachers could experience the online coursework and the resources available to them in small bites," he explains. "We found that teachers don't necessarily make use of free [online] resources unless they really understand how to use them first."

Tools being developed to help teachers take advantage of OPD sites are relatively easy to use but require some practice. Jing, for example, is a tool used by the Math Forum participants that allows scratch-work to be captured and saved, posted, or e-mailed by participants.

Another potential obstacle that has yet to be resolved is whether or how teachers should get in-service or PD credit for using OPD websites on their own. Thus far, there is no mechanism in place for assigning official credit for such use of portals or websites, unless it is a part of coursework for a district- or school-sanctioned course.

And some participating say the process lacks the human touch. Judith Hassel, a veteran Los Angeles English teacher, missed having face-to-face contact with her peers, even as she worked online with her classmates around California to assemble a research paper for a class on instructing English language learners. "I still wanted to meet my cohort after it was over," she says.

Still, this has not dissuaded her from considering other online courses. "Teachers are always learning, too, whether from each other or our own students," she concludes.

This chapter originally appeared in the January/February 2011 issue of the Harvard Education Letter.

FOR FURTHER INFORMATION

L.M. O'Dwyer et al. *e-Learning for Educators: Effects of Online Professional Development on Teachers and Their Students*. Chestnut Hill, MA: Technology and Assessment Study Collaborative (InTASC), 2010. Available online at www.bc.edu/research/intasc

About the Editor

Nancy Walser is the editor of the *Harvard Education Letter* and author of *The Essential School Board Book: Better Governance in the Age of Accountability* (Harvard Education Press, 2009). With Caroline Chauncey, Walser co-edited two previous books in the Spotlight Series, including *Spotlight on Student Engagement, Motivation, and Achievement* (Harvard Education Press, 2009) and *Spotlight on Leadership and School Change* (Harvard Education Press, 2007).

About the Contributors

Kristina Cowan is a freelance journalist with 14 years of experience covering a variety of beats including higher education, K–12 education, and career/workforce issues. She attended Northwestern University twice; first for a bachelor's degree in speech, and later for a master's degree in journalism. Cowan spent seven years in the Washington, D.C., area covering higher education for a trade publication, and congressional energy policy for a major news group. She lives in the Chicago area with her husband and son.

James Paul Gee is the Mary Lou Fulton Presidential Professor of Literacy Studies at Arizona State University. He is the author of numerous books including two editions of *What Video Games Have to Teach Us About Learning and Literacy* (2001, 2007) and, most recently, *Women and Gaming: The Sims and 21st Century Learning* (2010) and *Language and Learning in the Digital Age* (2011) with Elizabeth R. Hayes.

Colleen Gillard is a freelance journalist and *Harvard Education Letter* contributor. Gillard, who lives in Cambridge, Mass., has written for *Edutopia*, *The Boston Globe*, and *The San Francisco Chronicle*.

Will Richardson is a popular speaker, blogger (webblogged.org) and author on the topic of technology and education. The third edition of his bestselling book, *Blogs, Wikis, Podcasts, and Other Powerful Web Tools for the Classroom*, was published in 2010.

Robert Rothman is a senior fellow at the Alliance for Excellent Education in Washington, D.C. He is the former editor of *Voices in Urban Education*, a quarterly journal published by the Annenberg Institute for School Reform at Brown University.

Dave Saltman recently obtained his English and social science teaching credentials in California, where he also tutors in a public library literacy program for adults and youth. He spent the early part of his career writing for newspapers. He then went on to work as a producer, writer, and editor for Internet firms. He grew up outside Washington, D.C., and graduated with a B.A. in history from Clark University in Worcester, Mass. He lives in Los Angeles.

Brigid Schulte lives in Alexandria, Va., where she is a staff writer for the *Washington Post*. Schulte has written about desegregation and year-round schooling for the *Harvard Education Letter*.